TO ENCOURAGE YOU:

ESSAYS ON CHRISTIAN THEMES FOR HOPE AND WHOLENESS

CHARLES A. BARRETT

To Encourage You:
Essays on Christian Themes for Hope and Wholeness

Charles A. Barrett

To Encourage You: Essays on Christian Themes for Hope and Wholeness
Published by
CAB Publishing Company, LLC
PO Box 422
McLean, Virginia, 22101

ISBN-13: 978-0692051207
ISBN-10: 0692051201

ACKNOWLEDGEMENTS

The following individuals have been tremendously helpful to me in the completion of this project. Their insightful editorial feedback and suggestions from diverse theological and academic perspectives have made it a product that I am proud to share with you. I am grateful for their friendship and willingness to dedicate their time to this endeavor.

Rev. Dawn Armand
Mr. Nathan Fields
Jennifer Lieberman, PhD
Min. Johnnie Mae Parker
Rosalyn Pitts Clark, PhD
Mr. Dwayne Williams

I especially want to thank my wife, Lisa, whose unending love and support are inspiring, empowering, and encouraging. Thank you for understanding me. Thank you for thinking and planning with me. Thanks for listening to me talk, incessantly, about this book and my other ideas. I am able to create because of you.

CONTENTS

ACKNOWLEDGEMENTS   *v*
A LETTER FOR YOU   *ix*

HAPPY NEW YEAR   *ix*
The Year in Perspective: Implications for Victorious Christian Living   1
New Year, New Season: Begin with the End in Mind   7

RELATIONSHIPS   **13**
Pursuing God: Chasing After You   15
Reconciliation: The Restoration of Relationships   21
Reconciliation: The Restoration of Relationships, Part 2   27
Lessons from the Lake: Drifting   35

SPIRITUAL MATURITY   **41**
Do You Hear What I Hear?   43
The Truth About Numbers: Bigger and Better?   51
When God Says No   57

SPRING, LENT, AND EASTER   **65**
It's a New Season!   67
A Lenten Meditation: More of God and Less of Me   73
A Lenten Meditation: I Need More of You   81
Don't Forget to Remember: You Are Always on His Mind   87
Yes, Jesus Loves Me   91

ENCOURAGEMENT   **99**
My Grace is Sufficient: Black, Christian, and Living
with Mental Illness   101
To Encourage You: The Proper Perspective on Going Through   107
To Encourage You: The Other Side of Through   113

HAPPY FATHER'S DAY — 119
In Defense of Fathers — 121
If You Don't Father Them, Who Will? — 127
Good Good Father — 133

FREEDOM, PRIVILEGE, AND JUSTICE — 141
Independence Day: The Day He Set Me Free — 143
On Freedom, Privilege, and Justice — 149
Lest We Forget: The Tragedy of Moving on Too Quickly — 155
Can I Trust You? — 165

FOR STUDENTS AND EDUCATORS — 171
Behind the Scenes — 173
Altering Public Space — 177
Drowning in Shallow Water — 183
On Being a Misfit — 189

THANKSGIVING — 195
A Thanksgiving Meditation — 197
It Took All of That to Get to This — 203
Grateful for Grace — 211

END OF THE YEAR — 219
He Is Our Peace — 221
The Year In Review: Go Back Another Way — 227
Nevertheless — 233

ENDNOTES — 239

A LETTER FOR YOU

Dear Friend—

I am excited to share this collection of essays with you. Central to everything I do as a musician, teacher, writer, and psychologist is a desire to help people grow and experience the joy of hope and wholeness. And because spiritual growth is a process, where we find ourselves at any moment is less important than continuing to develop into the person that God desires us to be.

As you read this book, don't think of it as an ordinary text that should be completed within a few days or even a few weeks. Instead, think of it as a resource to encourage you along your spiritual journey. Thematically aligned to a calendar year, the essays will encourage you throughout the inevitable seasons of life. As you allow God to set your pace, take your time to read, and perhaps re-read, the entries as many times as you like. Most importantly, open your heart and mind to what the Lord will show you. At the risk of sounding cliché, I am confident that there is something uniquely for you in each piece. You will see that scripture references have been included throughout the collection; I encourage you to read these passages in a version of the Bible that you can easily understand. Unless otherwise noted, I have used the New Living Translation (NLT).

To support spiritual development, questions for personal reflection and meditation follow each of the relatively short entries. After reading each piece, I encourage you to spend a few moments in quiet reflection and perhaps journal your responses to the questions posed. While the corresponding questions have been designed for self-paced individual study, they can be easily adapted for use in small group settings. Such intimate gatherings are not only helpful for our own accountability, but learning and growing is also more fun when shared with others in authentic community.

As you read, reflect, and meditate, I pray that you will not only experience God's unwavering and unconditional love for you, but that you will learn more about yourself as you are becoming more like Christ.

Be encouraged.

We are in this together.

HAPPY
NEW YEAR

THE YEAR IN PERSPECTIVE: IMPLICATIONS FOR VICTORIOUS CHRISTIAN LIVING

For I know the plans I have for you, says the LORD.
They are plans for good and not for disaster, to give you a future and a hope.

Jeremiah 29: 11

It was November 1994, and the Reverend DeForest *Buster* Soaries, Jr. preached a simple, yet profound message based on the account of David and Goliath recorded in 1 Samuel 17. *The Power of a Proper Perspective* challenged believers to consider David's triumph over the giant as being inextricably connected to his perspective on God and the situation (vv. 45-47). In other words, David's perspective—one that was focused on the All-Powerful God and not intimidated by Goliath's physical presence—ultimately led to victory.

And so it is today. Having embarked upon a new year, in all that we do, let's develop and maintain the proper perspective by being mindful of these things.

INVITE THE LORD TO DWELL

At the beginning of the year, and each new day, it is fitting to intentionally invite the Lord to abide with us. As Paul reminded The Church at Corinth that their bodies were the temples of the Holy Spirit (1 Corinthians 6: 19), this is the most important place where God should be welcomed to take permanent residence. Further, The Church is more than man made structures of brick and mortar, but individuals—you and me—who comprise the living and breathing Body of Christ.

DECLARE AND LIVE BY FAITH

Make a declaration for what, by faith, is already done. And as we make these declarations, know that faith is not predicated on what can be discerned by our senses, but what is found in the Word of God. Fundamentally, living by faith involves believing what's been written in the pages of Genesis through Revelation although we might not understand everything. Further, because we believe God, our declarations aren't only reminders of the necessity of faith (Hebrews 11: 6), but also testaments that regardless of what we might experience throughout the year, we are more than conquerors through Jesus Christ who loves us (Romans 8:37)!

COVER EVERYTHING UNDER THE BLOOD

Exodus 12: 13: *But the blood on your doorposts will serve as a sign, marking the houses where you are staying. When I see the blood, I will pass over you...* Later in verses 24 through 27, the Israelites were charged to obey these instructions as a lasting ordinance for generations following. Because of this, there is no better way to place the year in proper perspective than by applying the blood—not of slain animals during the first Passover, but the final Sacrificial Lamb who died on Calvary—over our lives. Though weapons might be formed against us, they won't prosper. Why? Because we, and therefore every situation that we will face, have been covered under the blood!

REMAIN IN THE WILL OF GOD

One of my favorite passages of scripture is Luke 22: 42: *"Father, if you are willing, please take this cup of suffering away from me. Yet I want your will to be done, not mine."* This verse shows that Christ was honest with God: "Father, I don't want to go to the cross. And if there is any way that you can let me avoid this painful experience, please do it! But because I love you, and what you want is more important than anything—including my own comfort—what I want really doesn't matter. Whatever your will is, and whatever you want me to do, I will do it!" Coupled with being completely honest with God, more importantly, the text shows that we must ultimately grow to the place of total surrender and obedience to the will of God. For those of us who earnestly desire to please the Lord, wholeness and fulfillment will only be found in the will of God.

COUNT YOUR BLESSINGS

Thank God, in advance, for what you believe he will do throughout the year. Deliberately recalling the specific things that God has already done should lead to an eruption of praise and saying, "Thank you!"—two words that are not uttered enough in a culture of give me and give me more. But as we count our blessings, let's also establish a new precedent: a year in which our thanksgiving to God far outweighs our petitions of him.

MOVE FORWARD

Philippians 3: 12 through 14: *I don't mean to say that I have already achieved these things or that I have already reached perfection. But I press on to possess that perfection for which Christ Jesus first possessed me. No, dear brothers and sisters, I have not achieved it, but I focus on this one thing: Forgetting the past and looking forward to what lies ahead, I press on to reach the end of the race and receive the heavenly prize for which God, through Christ Jesus, is calling us.* In order to accomplish our goals, we must forget the mistakes, disappointments, missed opportunities, and setbacks of last year. Move forward knowing that each of those things is a distant memory.

Each of these principles will help us to place the year in proper perspective. Regardless of the circumstances and situations that we will inevitably encounter, we will be more than conquerors because we believe God can do exceedingly and abundantly above all that we can imagine (Ephesians 3: 20).

PERSONAL REFLECTION AND MEDITATION

1.   Use this space to write your thoughts and reflections on this essay.

2.   What was especially meaningful to you?

3.   What are some ways that you can move forward by forgetting your past mistakes and setbacks?

Thank you for another day. Thank you for everything that you will accomplish through me this year. Help me to remain focused on what you want me to do. When things are uncomfortable and inconvenient, and doubt tries to discourage me, thank you for increasing my faith to trust you more.

Amen.

NEW YEAR, NEW SEASON: BEGIN WITH THE END IN MIND

*Then the LORD said to me, Write my answer plainly on tablets, so
that a runner can carry the correct message to others. This vision is for
a future time. It describes the end, and it will be fulfilled.
If it seems slow in coming, wait patiently, for it will surely take place.
It will not be delayed.*

Habakkuk 2: 2-3

There is nothing magical about 12:00 on January 1ˢᵗ. Without purposing in our hearts and minds that our lives will be different, we run the risk of pouring old wine into new wineskins (Mark 2: 22). To this end, some of us might be familiar with *The Seven Habits of Highly Effective People* by noted businessman, Steven Covey (d. 2012). While each of his habits is important, Habit #2: *Begin With The End In Mind* is especially meaningful for this time of year.[1]

WRITE THE VISION AND MAKE IT PLAIN

Psalm 37: 4 could be one of the most misunderstood passages of scripture. Though the psalmist writes (paraphrasing) that if we delight ourselves in the Lord (spend quality time with God) he will give us the desires of our hearts, this does not mean that we will receive whatever we want. Instead, the text speaks to God giving us what our hearts should desire. In other words, he will place within us the things that we should pursue. Friends, this is central to our success this year.

Habakkuk 2: 2 & 3: *Write my answer plainly on tablets, so that a runner can carry the correct message to others. This vision is for a future time. It describes the end, and it will be fulfilled. If it seems slow in coming, wait patiently, for it will surely take place. It will not be delayed.* These verses are critical to all that God desires to accomplish in and through our lives. Specifically, before we can expect to do anything worthwhile, we must know what we are trying to accomplish. If we seek God—if we ask him to show us what he wants us to do—he will answer us. Further, he will give us instructions. Our responsibility, however, is to record everything that he says. We can't rely on our minds because we are prone to forget. And as the text suggests, the vision that the Lord gives us will have implications for others. Therefore, in order to effectively communicate the Lord's plan, write it down—literally. In a journal. In a notebook. In your phone. In your tablet. And after you've written it down, although it might take some time to be fulfilled, know that it will come to pass.

According to Covey, one of the best ways to incorporate Habit #2 into our lives is to develop a personal mission statement that focuses on what we want to be and do. Essentially, who am I? What am I about? What do I want to accomplish? If you haven't already, seek the Lord; wait for his response; and when he speaks to you, write what he says. Moreover, allow your life's mission statement to become the blueprint by which your aspirations become reality.

WORK BACKWARDS

As a school psychologist, I'm often involved with helping parents and teachers respond to a variety of academic and behavioral difficulties. Related to beginning with the end in mind, at times this means working backwards. Said another way, it includes establishing a goal and then identifying benchmarks that can be used to measure progress towards the goal. For example, if your goal is to write a book by the end of the year, what specific steps must be taken that also provide evidence of progress towards completing this project? Perhaps it's identifying a topic (January); outlining chapters 1, 2, and 3 (February); and drafting chapters 1, 2, and 3 (April). Parenthetically, not only does working backwards provide the accountability associated with specified due dates, but we are also less likely to be overwhelmed with having to complete a seemingly insurmountable undertaking at once.

BE FAITHFUL TO YOUR PLAN: IMPLEMENT IT WITH FIDELITY

In working with families and schools, there are often many good, if not great, interventions that have been developed to help children succeed. Why, then, aren't they achieving better outcomes? The answer, at times, is rather simple: the plan is not being implemented with fidelity. This is to say that there is nothing wrong with the plan but the manner in which it has, or has not, been carried out. Before discarding your plan because you think it is ineffective, consider this: have you been faithful to its design?

Success is not only about working harder, but smarter. And the best way to work smarter is to know precisely what we are working towards. If we know what we want to accomplish, all that we do necessarily rests on our response to the following question: Will doing this/these things bring me closer to accomplishing my goal(s)? If the answer is no, I pray that we will have the strength, courage, and discipline to no longer engage in these activities and/or with certain individuals. While there may not be anything inherently wrong with a certain activity or person, if they are not helping us to move closer to what we are trying to accomplish, they inevitably become distractions. In the words of Covey, "*If your ladder is not leaning against the right wall, every step you take gets you to the wrong place faster.*" [2]

Rather than wishing you a Happy New Year, I commend you to God, the Alpha and Omega—He who knows the end from the beginning.

PERSONAL REFLECTION AND MEDITATION

1. After spending some moments in reflection and meditation, identify 1-3 goals that you would like to accomplish this year.

   a. Goal #1

   b. Goal #2

   c. Goal #3

2. Identify a date (month, year) by which you would like to accomplish each goal.

Goal #1	Completion Date (month, year)
Goal #2	
Goal #3	

3. What specific steps do you have to take in order to accomplish your goals? The table below may help you organize your goals and action steps.

Goal	Completion Date (month, year)	Quarter 1 Activities: January through March	Quarter 2 Activities: April through June	Quarter 3 Activities: July through September	Quarter 4 Activities: October through December

RELATIONSHIPS

PURSUING GOD: CHASING AFTER YOU

As the deer longs for streams of water, so I long for you, O God.

Psalm 42: 1

*He's Just Not That into You*³ was a 2009 big screen adaptation of Greg Behrendt's and Liz Tuccillo's best-selling book, *He's Just Not That Into You: The No-Excuses Truth to Understanding Guys.*⁴ Depicting the dating misadventures of young adults, the film's message is conveyed through a character that is desperately trying to understand the mixed signals she continually receives from the men she meets. As both the book and film seek to warn their audiences of the signs that seemingly reveal whether or not someone is interested in a committed relationship with you, spiritually, this can be likened unto Isaiah 29: 13 (New English Translation): "*These people say they are loyal to me; they say wonderful things about me, but they are not really loyal to me...*" In other words, "They tell me what they think I want to hear but don't have any intention of being committed to me!" And though written from the perspective of women, the reverse is certainly applicable to men. Fellas, if she's not calling you; if she's not dating you; if she doesn't want to marry you; if she's married; or if she's selfish, she's just not that into you!

THE LESSON FROM PSALM 63: 1

O God, you are my God; I earnestly search for you. My soul thirsts for you; my whole body longs for you in this parched and weary land where there is no water. As thirst is often a powerful metaphorical illustration of longing for and desiring God, the spiritual significance of seeking him early shows that before we attempt anything else, or the day becomes filled with activities that are less important, we make a conscious decision to spend time with God because he is more important than anyone or anything. Friends, is starting your day by talking to God important? Have you made spending quality time with God a daily priority?

THE LESSON FROM JOSHUA 24: 14 & 15 and MATTHEW 6:24

Joshua 24: 14 and 15: *So fear the LORD and serve him wholeheartedly. Put away forever the idols your ancestors worshiped... Serve the LORD alone. But if you refuse to serve the LORD, then choose today whom you will serve.* Matthew 6: 24: *No one can serve two masters... You cannot serve both God and money.*

Through these passages, we learn that we have been created with free will—the capacity to make our own decisions. And although Joshua, as the spiritual leader of his family, declared that they would serve the Lord, each Israelite had to make his or her own decision. Friends, today, will you serve other gods—money, popularity—or the One, True, and Living God? At the heart of the matter is this: if we aren't committed to God, we are committed to someone or something else. What is taking the place of being totally committed to God? Is it the pursuit of wealth or some other artificial indicator of success? Perhaps it's a relationship with a man or woman that has taken the place that is reserved for God in your life? To whom or what are you committed that prevents you from being completely available to God?

THE LESSON FROM MATTHEW 16: 24

"...If any of you wants to be my follower, you must give up your own way, take up your cross, and follow me." Undeniably, true love is the most expensive gift that we will ever give to another. Further, it is much less about the person doing the loving than the one who is the object of the affection. Genuine love for God is no exception and will ultimately cost us our lives. Although Jesus paid it all, we owe him everything. Friends: are you willing to deny yourself—your pleasures and comforts—to follow God?

In the 12th verse of Proverbs 3 we learn that whom the Lord loves, he also corrects. But although he chastens us, we must always remember that whom the Lord loves, he also chases. Yes, God's love caused him to send his one and only son to die for our sins (John 3: 16); but such love is also demonstrated continuously. Recorded in Matthew 18: 12-14, *The Parable of the Lost Sheep* shows how deeply committed God is to his children. Although a man might have 100 sheep, if he loses one, his love for this lone sheep causes him to leave the 99 in pursuit of the one! And so it is with God: Because he loves us, he actively pursues us. Friends, although you say that you love God, are you pursuing him? And just in case you are worried about serving an elusive and evasive catch me if you can God, rest assured that when you earnestly seek him, you will find Him (Jeremiah 29: 13).

As in virtually every area of our lives, each of these lessons requires us to make a choice. If we don't hunger and thirst for God, it is because we have chosen not to do so. If we don't want to spend quality time with him, likewise, we have made this decision. Is your love for God such that it drives all that you do? Does your love for God cause you to always run towards him? Are you into God?

Regardless of your response, remember this: God is into you.

PERSONAL REFLECTION AND MEDITATION

1. Which aspect(s) of your life (e.g., things and/or people) have become more important than your relationship with God?

2. How can you make spending quality time with God a priority in your life? For some people, having a dedicated time each day for prayer, reflection, or meditation is helpful for them to consistently spend quality time with God.

3. If you are not currently spending quality time when God on a regular basis, I encourage you to do this for only 5 minutes each day. Try it for a few weeks. In fact, I have been told that it takes about 21 days for behavior change to happen. Remember that it's not about the amount of time (quantity), but the quality of time that you spend with God by giving him your undivided attention that is most important.

Thank you for loving me and for pursuing me. Help me to love you, faithfully, and to always make my relationship with you a priority. Amen.

RECONCILIATION: THE RESTORATION OF RELATIONSHIPS

God blesses those who work for peace, for they will be called the children of God.

Matthew 5: 9

Fundamentally, humans are relational beings. For this reason, from both Biblical (Genesis 2: 18) and psychological perspectives, it is unhealthy and unnatural for people to be alone. In fact, **Abraham Maslow's Hierarchy of Needs** suggests that the Need for Love and Belongingness is universal to the human condition. Despite occasionally craving moments of solitude away from everyone and everything, we yearn to be included, loved, valued, and accepted by others. As young children develop their social skills by learning to share, take turns, and eventually appreciate perspectives that are different from their own, regardless of our developmental maturity, we will always be faced with the challenging task of negotiating and nurturing relationships.

As the contemporary presentation of the Gospel message often includes motifs that are centered on the restoration of material things, although there is nothing inherently wrong with this idea, have we neglected reconciliation: the restoration of broken relationships? What does it mean to reconcile: *to restore friendly relations between* or *to settle [a disagreement]*? Despite knowing that we should live peaceably amongst our sisters and brothers (Matthew 5: 9; Hebrews 12: 14), what are some hindrances to reconciliation?

HINDRANCE #1: PRIDE

Pride, in the words of Bishop Norman Lyons, is *preoccupation with I and my*. Especially for men, whether we admit it or not, we are overly concerned with our image and the manner in which others perceive us. But while pride is not always a liability, it becomes costly when it gets in the way of doing what we know is pleasing to God. Pride obstructs reconciliation when our actions are inconsistent with humility and grace in order to uphold a façade of how we want to be viewed by others. While the truth of God's word says that we need to be reconciled to one another, pride responds with *does this make me look weak?* While truth says that reconciliation is necessary, pride makes excuses to avoid this very important work.

HINDRANCE #2: FEAR

Especially for men, we have been conditioned to be fearless. And if not fearless, we have been reinforced for not letting others know that we, at times, are afraid. As a man and as a psychologist, such thinking is both antiquated and counterproductive. Contrary to what many might believe, fear is not synonymous with weakness and it certainly is not the antithesis of masculinity and manhood. Concerning reconciliation, fear asks *how will others respond to my attempts for reconciliation?* Or, *do they even want to be reconciled to me?* Despite being based in a legitimate human emotion, fear that gives way to excessive nervousness, worry, and anxiety can become a paralyzing force that works in opposition to reconciliation.

HINDRANCE #3: HURT

Regardless of what you've been told, either as a man or about men, we hurt. In fact, because men have feelings like everyone else, we are susceptible to being hurt, especially by those whom we care about the most. So, what happens when men have been hurt by their friends, employers, wives, significant others, and even their children? Almost instinctively, we retreat in order to protect ourselves from further hurt and disappointment. And while this defense mechanism is understandable to some degree, hurt feelings can develop into a hardened heart that is not open to reconciliation. Like each of the hindrances, knowing whether hurt is preventing us from being reconciled to others is unique to the individual. For this reason, we must remain open to the Holy Spirit who, if we are listening, will help us to grow beyond our pain, which ultimately is necessary for reconciliation.

HINDRANCE #4: IMPATIENCE

Like other things in our lives, we want reconciliation to happen immediately. Unfortunately, because reconciliation almost always involves forgiveness, it is a process that takes time. In fact, because the place in which we find ourselves that makes reconciliation necessary likely did not happen overnight, the restoration of broken relationships will inevitably require patience.

HINDRANCE #5: LACK OF VULNERABILITY

Perhaps one of the most frustrating aspects of reconciliation is the realization that we are not responsible for other people's decisions. Said another way, reconciliation is challenging because of the myriad unknown variables that are associated with being vulnerable. For example, after we apologize or share how certain situations were hurtful, how will others respond to such transparency? Perhaps as a combination of pride, fear, and hurt, the reluctance to being vulnerable is rooted in the following: *Is this going to work? Will my attempts at reconciliation be received? How will I look after I bare my innermost feelings about things that hurt me?* But because we cannot control others' actions, we also cannot allow ourselves to not be vulnerable at the expense of actively pursuing reconciliation.

Friends, I pray that we would recognize these five realities of reconciliation. And because grace is always greater, let's allow it to work in and through us to actively pursue reconciliation.

PERSONAL REFLECTION AND MEDITATION

1. Which relationship (or relationships) needs to be restored in your life?

2. As you think about this relationship (or relationships), which of the hindrances (i.e., pride, fear, hurt, impatience, or lack of vulnerability) are standing in the way of reconciliation? Perhaps there are other hindrances that are preventing restoration and reconciliation in your relationships. If so, what are they?

3. Ask the Lord to show you how to work through these feelings so that relationships can be restored in your life. Use this space to write what he shows you.

Thank you for giving me the grace and strength to work through feelings of pride, fear, hurt, impatience, and lack of vulnerability so that relationships can be restored in my life.

Amen.

RECONCILIATION: THE RESTORATION OF RELATIONSHIPS, PART 2

Work at living in peace with everyone…

Hebrews 12: 14

Having focused on five realities that are associated with reconciliation, it is fitting to turn our attention to how relationships can be restored in our lives.

RECONCILIATION IS ACTIVE

It has been said that anything worth having requires work; and this truth applies to relationships. Whether between friends, siblings, spouses, parents and their children, or even neighbors, the same determination and commitment that we invest in earning advanced degrees, securing better jobs, and improving our financial situations is necessary to nurture healthy relationships. More than a trendy social media hashtag, #relationshipgoals are much too significant to be accomplished casually. We must be intentional about doing things that will ultimately make these aspirations realities.

For this reason, reconciliation is an active process that requires deliberate effort. Because God loves us, and desires a personal, intimate, and meaningful relationship with each of us, he pursues us.

Through the lens of three parables in Luke 15—*The Lost Sheep, The Lost Coin,* and *The Lost Son*—Jesus provides clear examples of active reconciliation. In the parable of *The Lost Sheep* (vv. 3-7), a man who has 100 sheep, but is missing one, *leaves* 99 in order to search for the one that is lost (v. 4). Metaphorically, this is what God does for each of us: he pursues us. Similarly, in the parable of *The Lost Coin* (vv. 8-10), a woman *searches high and low* until she finds the one that is missing. It does not matter that she has nine others; she is more concerned about, and committed to, the one coin that is lost! Last, the parable of *The Lost Son* (vv. 11-21) is the story of a young man who left his father's house to engage in what some might consider risky behavior (v. 13). But after experiencing what he thought was the good life, he came to his senses and wanted to return home (vv. 17-19). Verse 20: *"…And while he was still a long way off, his father saw him coming. Filled with love and compassion, he ran to his son, embraced him, and kissed him."* Friends, this is the active and intentional quality of reconciliation: although the young man chose to leave his father's house, reconciliation was more important than who was right or wrong. Even today, is being reconciled to friends and family members more important than justifying that you were right and they were wrong?

RECONCILIATION IS INCONVENIENT

But not only is reconciliation active, it is also inconvenient. Hebrews 12: 14: *Work at living in peace with everyone, and work at living a holy life, for those who are not holy will not see the Lord.* As a child, I remember hearing this scripture in various charismatic settings. Often employing the poetic eloquence of the King James Version, the emphasis was not placed on *follow peace with all men,* but rather *holiness, without which no man shall see the Lord.* But as I've matured, I have come to realize that holiness is not the only, or even the most difficult, challenge of living a life that is pleasing to God. Instead, living peaceably amongst those whom I encounter every day warrants closer attention. Not to be overlooked, the text does not differentiate between those with whom we should live peaceably. In other words, we must seek to live at peace with everyone—even those who do not like us, fundamentally disagree with us, and routinely challenge us.

Similarly, Matthew 5: 9 contains these words: *"God blesses those who work for peace, for they will be called the children of God."* As Jesus spoke to a rowdy, motley crew who would later be instrumental in forever changing the world, he outlined the essential attributes of being one of his followers. Known as The Beatitudes (Matthew 5: 3-12), among other things, he admonished them to be humble (v. 5), merciful (v. 7), to have a pure heart (v. 8), and to work for peace (v. 9). Importantly, let's consider verses 10 and 11: *"God blesses those who are persecuted for doing right, for the Kingdom of Heaven is theirs. God blesses you when people mock you and persecute you and lie about you and say all sorts of evil things against you because you are my followers."* In other words, as reconciliation will not happen without intentionality, actively pursuing peace will inevitably be costly and inconvenient.

Like many of the disciples, some of these traits are likely not within our nature. Especially related to being a peacemaker, socially constructed gender stereotypes have not encouraged men to behave in this manner. But regardless of the ways in which we have been conditioned to conduct ourselves, the power and presence of the Holy Spirit can help us to mature and develop the qualities that are lacking so that we can become all that God desires us to be (Galatians 5: 22-23). In fact, the times in which we are living present numerous opportunities to practice reconciliation. As we witness increasingly hostile tensions between nations, and more accurately, between ethnicities (Matthew 24: 7) both in the United States and around the world, how do we pursue peace? Simply stated, one person at a time. As depicted in Luke 15, we pursue individuals, one at a time. We talk to our neighbors, one at a time. We engage with those who think differently than we do, one at a time. We intentionally and deliberately build community so that we can grow from sharing our stories and lived experiences.

A PERFECT METAPHOR FOR RECONCILIATION

Several years ago, Oprah Winfrey ended her interviews by asking a simple, yet profound question: *What do you know for sure?* While I can think of several responses, I am particularly certain of this: God uses relationships as his primary method of developing our Christian character and accomplishing his plan for our lives.

Even before I was married, I often wondered why marriage is the metaphor used to illustrate God's relationship with us, his Church (Ephesians 5). And through my relatively short experience as a husband, I have learned, firsthand, why marriage is the best possible example and demonstration of Christ's love for, and commitment toward, us. Fundamentally, marriage is the union of two imperfect people who desire to become connected and united as one in every way (Genesis 2: 24). Like reconciliation, the process of becoming one requires intentionality and, at times, will be inconvenient. Nevertheless, the magic and mystery of marriage lies in inherently flawed individuals striving to perfect their union through unconditional love and undying commitment. Through good days and bad, happy and sad, marriage is continual reconciliation. It is patience that never grows weary with impatience. It is forgiveness that never grows tired of forgiving. The marriage covenant embodies unyielding grace, which is the cornerstone of reconciliation: experiencing that which we don't deserve and extending the same to others.

Whether married or not, each of us can learn from this sacred institution. Are we allowing grace to govern our relationships? Are we allowing grace to guide our decisions and actions? Having been the recipients of grace, are we instruments of the same? Although inconvenient, are we actively pursuing peace and reconciliation with all people?

Today, what are you doing to restore relationships in your life?

PERSONAL REFLECTION AND MEDITATION

1. Use this space to write your thoughts and reflections on this essay.

2. What was especially meaningful to you?

3. How can you actively pursue reconciliation or the restoration of a relationship with at least one person?

Thank you for pursuing me. Help me to pursue peace with others. Give me the strength and patience to engage with those who think differently I do. Help me to intentionally build authentic community so that I can learn from others and grow as a person by listening to the stories and lived experiences of my neighbors.

Amen.

LESSONS FROM THE LAKE: DRIFTING

Trust in the Lord with all your heart; do not depend on your own understanding. Seek his will in all you do, and he will show you which path to take.

Proverbs 3: 5-6

Growing up in a coastal town on the South Shore of Long Island, I have always been fascinated by water. Even today, my #lifegoals include owning a waterfront home, coupled with jet skis and a boat on which I plan to begin and end most of my days. But while the sound of waves crashing against the shore has a calming effect on us, water can also devastate communities and wreak havoc in our lives. In other words, despite its soothing and almost therapeutic qualities, we should never underestimate the strength of water.

Each summer, my family and I enjoy kayaking on a nearby lake. One particular Sunday afternoon, it occurred to me that although I wasn't paddling, I was still moving. Eventually, I realized that I was a considerable distance from where I began. Although drifting on the lake was quite peaceful, floating aimlessly through life has dire consequences. After beginning in one place, but finding ourselves in unsafe and unhealthy situations that we had never imagined, we often wonder how these things happened.

DRIFTING IS SUBTLE

Because rivers, streams, oceans and lakes are constantly moving, if we're not careful, water can cause us to drift from where we expect to be. Moreover, big problems aren't always necessary to take us away; seemingly little things are enough.

It is safe to assume that most married couples intend to enjoy happy and fruitful lives with their spouses and want their relationships to last forever. However, many marriages end in divorce. Although there are a numerous explanations for this phenomenon, divorce is typically not the result of deliberate offenses that have been committed by insensitive and uncaring husbands and wives. Instead, divorce is the byproduct of little things that have ballooned into significant challenges for the couple. Rather than heeding the wisdom of Ephesians 4: 26, it's the result of a few hours, which becomes several days, of not speaking to one another. It's the result of a few weeks, which turns into several months, of not spending quality time together. In the moment, these things are seemingly inconsequential and are often ignored. But over time, distance is growing between two people who once committed themselves to loving each other unconditionally. Albeit subtle, slowly, yet surely, couples are drifting farther and farther apart.

DRIFTING IS THE ABSENCE OF PURPOSE

As couples need to be aware of, and responsive to, the little things that are causing them to drift apart, we also need a clear vision for our lives. Where do we want to be in six months? What do we want to accomplish in five years? Not only should we consider these questions as individuals, but they are also necessary for the health and strength of our marriages and families. Although not thinking about where I wanted to be while relaxing on the lake was rather enjoyable and I simply found myself on the far side of the water, wandering through life without purpose is dangerous and has far reaching and life changing implications.

It has been said that if we don't stand for something, we will fall for anything. As couples who aren't intentional about communicating or spending quality time together will inevitably drift apart, casually experiencing life without knowing what we want, where we want to be, or how we should achieve our goals leads to passively accepting whatever comes our way and wherever we find ourselves.

DRIFTING IS THE ABSENCE OF RELATIONSHIP

Despite some of us being introverted or shy by nature, humans are relational beings who crave meaningful connections with others. While on the lake, I realized that drifting often happens when we're alone. Two scriptures are particularly fitting in this regard. First, Proverbs 27: 17: *As iron sharpens iron, so a friend sharpens a friend.* Similarly, Ecclesiastes 4: 9-12:

> *Two people are better off than one, for they can help each other succeed. If one person falls, the other can reach out and help. But someone who falls alone is in real trouble. Likewise, two people lying close together can keep each other warm. But how can one be warm alone? A person standing alone can be attacked and defeated, but two can stand back-to-back and conquer. Three are even better, for a triple-braided cord is not easily broken.*

Like the early New Testament Church that is chronicled in the Book of Acts and remains the exemplar of Christian community (Acts 2: 42-47), these passages underscore the fact that we were not created to live in isolation. As people, but also members of the Body of Christ, we are interdependent on one another (1 Corinthians 12: 12-27). In fact, relationships are so important that God uses them to perfect our Christian character and mold us into the people that he wants us to be. We learn to love through relationship, and we learn to be kind by interacting with others. Similarly, patience and self-control can only be developed by living and working with those who compel us to exercise these qualities (Galatians 5: 22-23).

Because drifting is subtle, we're often unaware that we are moving farther from where we should be until it's too late. For this reason, relationships are not only comforting, but they're also protective. And although they require commitment and effort to be cultivated, the beauty of relationship is that while we're on the water of life, seemingly resting but really drifting into perilous predicaments, we have someone to help us. Yes, we're never alone (Psalm 46: 1; Psalm 139: 7-12; John 14: 16); but sometimes we need the physical presence of another person who will walk with us and hold our hand as we experience life's most difficult seasons.

Instead of drifting without purpose, be encouraged with Proverbs 3: 5-6: *Trust in the Lord with all your heart; do not depend on your own understanding. Seek his will in all you do, and he will show you which path to take.* As we spend quality time with God, he will show us what we should be pursuing.

PERSONAL REFLECTION AND MEDITATION

1. Spend some moments reflecting on whether you know the purpose that God has for your life. If you don't know your purpose in life, ask God to show you. Use this space to write your purpose.

2. How can you be more intentional about developing healthy relationships with your relatives, children, and/or spouse?

3. Through the lens of Proverbs 27: 17 and Ecclesiastes 4: 9-12, identify at least one person to whom you can be accountable in life.

Thank you that my life has purpose. Help me to live in a way that always brings me closer to fulfilling your purpose for my life. Amen.

SPIRITUAL
MATURITY

DO YOU HEAR WHAT I HEAR?

Samuel did not yet know the LORD because he had never had a message from the LORD before. So the LORD called a third time, and once more Samuel got up and went to Eli. "Here I am. Did you call me?" Then Eli realized it was the LORD who was calling the boy. So he said to Samuel, "Go and lie down again, and if someone calls again, say, 'Speak, LORD, your servant is listening...'"

1 Samuel 3: 7-9

God is always speaking; but sometimes he speaks in unconventional ways. As he used unlikely examples to teach us profound lessons (John 4: 7-27; Luke 7: 36-50), let's consider how he can speak to us through the writings of Theodor Seuss Geisel, also known as Dr. Seuss. Without spoiling the plot of *Horton Hears a Who*, it's essentially an allegory about an eccentric elephant that hears a voice coming from a tiny speck of dust.[5] As the story unfolds, he is ridiculed and ostracized for believing in what no one else does.

WHEN DOES GOD SPEAK TO US?

"On the 15th of May, in the Jungle of Nool, in the heat of the day, in the cool of the pool, he was splashing... enjoying the jungle's great joys... when Horton the elephant heard a small noise."[6] Horton's life changed while he was doing something—even if it was simply taking a bath. As the tiny speck represents God's still, small voice (1 Kings 19: 12), this reminds me of how the Lord called David and anointed him to be king—while he was tending his father's sheep (1 Samuel 16: 11-13)—and when the birth of Baby Jesus was revealed to the often forgotten and marginalized shepherds—while they were busy, working, in the fields (Luke 2: 8-16).

HOW DO WE KNOW THAT GOD IS SPEAKING TO US?

Because God will never force us to do anything, he often speaks softly, or as we tell children in school, using his inside voice. But after God speaks (calls us), like Horton, we are responsible for responding (answering).

Another pivotal character in Seuss' story is the Sour Kangaroo. Released by 20th Century Fox in 2008, the animated film describes her as "the type who's convinced she knows better than you. She made every law and enforced every rule… a self-proclaimed head of the Jungle of Nool." As such, the Sour Kangaroo challenged Horton the most by asserting: "…if you can't see, hear, or feel something, it doesn't exist!"[7]

If a tree falls in the forest and no one is around to hear it, does it make a sound? Similarly, if a person does not hear the voice of the Lord, does it mean that God is not speaking? The most appropriate conclusion that can be made from the kangaroo's statement is this: if you can't see, hear, or feel something, it simply means that you can't see, hear, or feel it! So, if you can't hear the voice of the Lord, you simply cannot hear it. Whether or not we can discern what God is saying does not change the fact that he is indeed speaking (1 Corinthians 2: 14). Horton challenges the Sour Kangaroo to acknowledge that there is a voice coming from the tiny speck. Whereas she argues that the speck is too small to have people speaking on it, Horton is not focused on the size of the speck, but his own size. He says these words: *Maybe they aren't small. Maybe we're big.* In other words, it's not that God isn't speaking, but rather we impede our ability to hear what he is saying. Friends, what could be preventing us from hearing God clearly?

WHY DOES GOD SPEAK TO US?

Horton hears "…a very faint yelp as if some tiny person were calling for help." As a result, he is compelled to save this person living on the speck of dust. Friends, like Horton, there are people whose lives are dependent on our obedience to what God says. For example, Noah built a boat that saved his family and animals after a great flood destroyed the earth (Genesis 6-8; Genesis 7: 23). In the same manner that Horton was the only one who knew that life existed in a microscopic world, there are things that only you can accomplish. Friends, if you don't [insert what God has given you to do], who will?

DON'T ALLOW ANYONE TO TAKE WHAT GOD HAS SPOKEN TO YOU

Despite the negativity of the Sour Kangaroo, Horton refused to deny what he heard coming from the tiny speck. From the moment it flew by his ear, he chased it. He pursued it. Although there were obstacles, he was faithful to it. Horton was not going to lose sight of what he heard!

In John 10: 10, Jesus says these words: *The thief's purpose is to steal and kill and destroy. My purpose is to give them a rich and satisfying life.* Although one interpretation of this passage is that the enemy exists to steal us, to kill us, and to destroy us, another perspective is that he wants to thwart the word of God that lives inside of us. In other words, he wants the promise that God has given us. Because the word can change every situation, like Horton looked after the speck, we, too, must protect that which we know the Lord has spoken to us.

DESPITE THEIR REACTION, TELL THEM

The cry from the speck is likely Ned McDodd, the mayor of Who-ville. Similar to Horton, his eventual hero, the mayor is living amongst people who mock him for what he believes. Nevertheless, Horton and the mayor told others what they knew to be true because lives were dependent on such radical faith and persistent obedience.

In Jeremiah 26, we read that there is always a consequence associated with the Lord speaking to us. Verse 2: *"…Stand in the courtyard in front of the Temple of the LORD, and make an announcement to the people who have come there to worship from all over Judah. Give them my entire message; include every word."* Although Jeremiah was obedient (vv. 4-7), what he said was not popular (vv. 8-11). Like the mayor and Horton, it can be uncomfortable when the Lord speaks to us because what we need to communicate is not always appealing or convenient. Like those to whom Jeremiah spoke, the residents of Who-ville felt that they were living just fine. Although their motto was "we have all that we need and need all we have," unknowingly, they were in serious danger…

As Horton and the mayor engaged in continuous dialogue, God wants a personal relationship with each of us, which includes consistent and meaningful communication.   And just like a person's a person no matter how small, a word [from God] is a word, no matter how small.

PERSONAL REFLECTION AND MEDITATION

1. Use this space to write your thoughts and reflections on this essay.

2. What was especially meaningful to you?

3. Because God speaks to each of us differently, do you know how he speaks to you? For some he speaks through situations that we encounter in life. For others he speaks through dreams. If you don't know how God speaks to you, ask him to show you.

Thank you for speaking to me. Help me to always recognize your voice. Give me the strength and courage to listen and act on what you say to me. Amen.

THE TRUTH ABOUT NUMBERS:
BIGGER AND BETTER?

*Never forget that it was one shepherd boy musician, who was also the
youngest of his brothers, who fought and killed a giant. It was a little boy's
lunch of five loaves and two fish that fed a multitude of more than 5,000.
And most importantly, it was one man, with a motley crew of
12 disciples, who forever changed the course of history.*

What does it mean to be significant? To better understand this idea, we can
borrow terms from applied research. Whereas statistical significance refers to
results that are mathematically meaningful, clinical significance is the degree to
which outcomes have life changing implications. Through the lens of Judges 7,
let's look closer at the relationship between numbers and significance.

THE BIBLICAL PRECEDENT

Judges 7 shows that numbers don't matter to God and are of no consequence
for his divine plan. A paraphrased version of Judges 7: 2 might be said this way:
"If all of these men fight, then Israel will think that it was by their own strength
and power that they were victorious over their enemies." So to use a term from
the sports world, God made the first cut—an astounding 22,000—by dismiss-
ing those who were fearful (v. 3). But because the remaining 10,000 were still
too many, he cut another 9,700 when he told Gideon to send home everyone
except those who *lap the water with their tongues as a dog* (vv. 4-7).

GOD MUST ASSEMBLE HIS TEAM

Having assembled his team, the Lord told the Israelites that they were going to
be victorious (v. 7) despite the multitude that they were facing (v. 12). Consider this: it was after the Lord brought together those whom he wanted that
Gideon and the army were positioned for success. In the same manner, until
our teams only include those that satisfy the necessary requirements (e.g., work

ethic, commitment, discipline), we will not accomplish what God desires us to achieve.

FAITH OVER FEAR

Although I used to think that faith was the opposite of fear, more accurately, faith is the triumph over fear. Bishop Neil Ellis says it this way: "a faith that has not been tested is a faith that cannot be trusted." Friends, our faith must be stronger than the uncertainty that we will inevitably face as a function of our humanity, especially when pursuing new opportunities in unchartered territory. Notice that the 22,000 fearful men that were dismissed from the Israelite army (Judges 7: 3) was the largest cut that was made. Could it be that the primary reason some people are not qualified to work with you is that they are fearful—making decisions according to what they see rather than living by faith (2 Corinthians 5: 7)?

THE CENTRALITY OF OBEDIENCE

The success experienced by Gideon and the Israelites was directly related to their obedience. As shown in verses 17 through 22 of Judges 7, God always provides specific instructions, which if followed, leads to a favorable outcome. For this reason, the victory actualized in verse 22 was quite similar to the events recorded in 2 Chronicles 20. As Gideon and those with him did not engage in a natural fight (Judges 7: 22), when Jehoshaphat sent Judah (musicians and singers) ahead of the army (2 Chronicles 20: 21), their enemies destroyed themselves (vv. 22-23). In both instances, though outnumbered (2 Chronicles 20: 1-2), the Israelites prevailed because of their obedience to God.

THE UNITY PRINCIPLE

Judges 7: 22 (New International Version): *when the three hundred trumpets sounded...*—when everyone who was on the team followed Gideon's instructions—*...the LORD caused the men throughout the camp to turn on each other with their swords.* More than the size of the crowd, God will supernaturally manifest his presence when we are united for a single cause (Psalm 133; 2 Chronicles 5: 13-14; Acts 2: 1-4).

THE VISION DRIVES THE DESIGN

In graduate school, my professors ingrained in me the following mantra: *What is the research question?* It is a principle that cannot be avoided: every aspect of a research study is driven by, determined by, and governed by the research question.

In virtually every aspect of our culture, bigger is erroneously synonymous with better. With social media, we measure our worth by the number of Facebook friends or followers on Twitter and Instagram as if these metrics make us more legitimate. But numbers don't necessarily determine significance. In the spirit of research design, what is the research question? Said another way, what is the vision? What has God given you to accomplish? What is your assignment? And after knowing these things, what do you need in order to be effective? As we learned from Judges 7, rest assured that effectiveness is not predicated on numbers. In fact, there could be too many people involved. Statistically speaking, almost anything becomes significant with enough people. If 10,000 protesters are marching in a certain city, the purpose of their demonstration can easily be overshadowed by the number of people taking over a major thoroughfare, which allows them to be noticed (e.g., media coverage) and seemingly legitimizes their cause. Size, therefore, can be a distraction.

Friends, don't be discouraged when you see others with larger followings than you might currently have. Don't assume that bigger houses and greater sums of money are synonymous with effectiveness. In fact, the adage that says *there is strength in numbers* does not mean that every person in the number should be in the number. As important as numbers are for defensible reasons, we should only be concerned with answering the following questions: what has God called me to do and what is necessary to accomplish the vision?

Never forget that it was one shepherd boy musician, who was also the youngest of his brothers, who fought and killed a giant (1 Samuel 16: 11-13; 1 Samuel 17: 49-51). It was a little boy's lunch of five loaves and two fish that fed a multitude of more than 5,000 (Mark 6: 41-44). And most importantly, it was one man, with a motley crew of 12 disciples, who forever changed the course of history (Matthew 1: 21; John 3: 16-17).

PERSONAL REFLECTION AND MEDITATION

1. Returning to *New Year, New Season: Begin with the End in Mind* (p. 7), what are your goals? How are you doing with making progress towards your goals?

2. If you have been implementing your plan faithfully and things are not working, what adjustments should you make?

3. If working with certain individuals is necessary for you to accomplish your goals, what specific steps can you take to make sure that you are only working with the right people?

Thank you for not measuring my worth by my followers or material possessions. Help me to remain focused on what you have called me to do despite the world's metrics of success. Amen.

WHEN GOD SAYS NO

"If we are thrown into the blazing furnace, the God whom we serve is able to save us. He will rescue us from your power, Your Majesty. But even if he doesn't, we want to make it clear to you, Your Majesty, that we will never serve your gods or worship the gold statue you have set up."

Daniel 3: 17-18

In recent years, an increasingly popular trend in American public education has been the affect of positive methods on children's behavior. The widespread acceptance of this approach has led entire school systems to implement programs such as Positive Behavioral Interventions and Supports (PBIS) to improve children's social, emotional, and behavioral functioning. As its name suggests, PBIS involves teaching youngsters to behave in a prosocial manner by using positive rather than negative terminology. For example, the punitive directive of *no running in the hallways* becomes positively phrased as *use walking feet*. Rather than saying *no talking in the library*, children are expected to *use quiet voices*. Very importantly, coupled with these behavioral expectations is a reward—a token that reinforces the desired expression and makes it more likely to continue.

While it cannot be denied that positive approaches have been effective in reducing disciplinary infractions, they are also not without their critics. One of the most popular points of contention challenging this contemporary concept rests on the following question: *What is wrong with telling children no?* For several reasons, including generational, cultural, and philosophical differences, not all parents and teachers support the exclusive use of positive methods to effectively manage children's behavior. To these individuals, *no* is a necessary reality that children must be taught to understand.

Friends, what happens when God says no?

REMEMBER THE THREE HEBREW BOYS?

One of the most masterfully crafted literary sentences can be found in Charles Dickens' *A Tale of Two Cities:*

> It was the best of times, it was the worst of times, it was the age of wisdom, it was the age of foolishness, it was the epoch of belief, it was the epoch of incredulity, it was the season of Light, it was the season of Darkness, it was the spring of hope, it was the winter of despair, we had everything before us, we had nothing before us, we were all going direct to Heaven, we were all going direct the other way.[8]

Although the opening to a classic novel, it is also an appropriate metaphor for life, especially the Christian life. No doubt, the great things that God does for us are symbolic of *the best of times.* But let us never forget that between these victories are moments experiencing *the worst of times.*

A perfect illustration of this dichotomy is captured throughout the first three chapters of Daniel, a book whose theological theme is centered on God's sovereignty. In chapter 1, several events suggest that for Daniel and his friends—Shadrach, Meshach, and Abednego—it was, indeed, the best of times. Despite their home being taken over by King Nebuchadnezzar (v. 1), they were amongst the most attractive and intelligent young men who were selected to be educated in the ways of Babylon, after which they would be assigned to work for the king (vv. 3-5). In 21st century terms, these young men participated in an exclusive training program, which had the promise of job security and extraordinary benefits. Continuing into chapter 2, because of the gift that God had given Daniel to interpret dreams (v. 47), he was rewarded with a *high position* (v. 48) and his friends were also promoted in their responsibilities (v. 49). For these Hebrew boys, it was the best of times.

But the peace and prosperity of these young men's lives was viciously challenged in chapter 3. The experience of Shadrach, Meshach, and Abednego in the fiery furnace begins with King Nebuchadnezzar constructing an image (v. 1) that he commanded everyone to worship (vv. 4-5). Moreover, he was very clear about the consequences of not adhering to this decree (v. 6). While most people followed the king's instructions (v. 7), Shadrach, Meshach, and Abednego did not (v. 12) and were subsequently interrogated by Nebuchadnezzar about their decision (vv. 14-15). Despite what these young men were facing, verses 16, 17, and 18 (New International Version) are particularly significant:

> *Shadrach, Meshach and Abednego replied to him, "King Nebuchadnezzar, we do not need to defend ourselves before you in this matter. If we are thrown into the blazing furnace, the God we serve is able to deliver us from it, and he will deliver us from Your Majesty's hand. But even if he does not, we want you to know, Your Majesty, that we will not serve your gods or worship the image of gold you have set up."*

This seemingly impossible situation for the young Israelites continues with the fiery furnace being made to be seven times hotter than usual (v. 19), being tied up by the strongest soldiers in the Babylonian army (v. 20), and ultimately thrown into the furnace (vv. 21, 23). For Shadrach, Meshach, and Abednego, no doubt, it seemed to be the worst of times.

REASONS FOR NO

Verses 17 and 18 underscore a subtle, yet important, theological truth. Although they were facing a fatal situation, these young men were confident in whom and what they believed: God and his sovereignty—regardless of if he delivered them from the fiery furnace. Coupled with verse 16, the passage shows that they were open to being spared from the agonizing misery, which was supposed to be their punishment for disobeying the king's decree. But what was God's response? Based on verses 21 and 23, he said *no*. Why would God, who says that he loves us unconditionally, say *no*? Could it be that God's *no* is difficult to grasp and even more uncomfortable to accept because we live in an egocentric culture that is filled with individuals who seem to be offended when they are denied access to what they want? If we are not careful, such an attitude can influence what we expect from our relationship with God: *he is supposed to say yes to everything that I ask.*

But when God says *no,* fundamentally it is because his ways are not like our ways (Isaiah 55: 8-9). In other words, he does not think like we do neither does he see things in the ways that we see them. Further, when God says *no* it's because his plan far exceeds what we can ever hope for ourselves. And very importantly, because *no* is not necessarily synonymous with disapproval, we should not assume that God is displeased with us.

As some believe that telling children *no* is healthy for their development, God's *no* is necessary for our spiritual maturity. First, it helps us to develop our Christian character (Galatians 5: 22-23) as we learn to accept that what we want might not be what's best or consistent with God's perfect plan. Consider the end of Jesus' prayer in Luke 22: 42 (English Standard Version): "*...nevertheless not my will, but yours, be done...*" Paraphrased, "Although I want you to do this for me, I will accept no if what I want is not what you want," how many of us could pray with such a mindset? Next, God's *no* is an opportunity for him to show us who he says he is and who we say we want him to be. When we are faced with various challenges and God does not respond in the manner in which we think he should, how would we know that he never gives us more than we can handle (1 Corinthians 10: 13)? In fact, if God had miraculously rescued the Hebrew boys from the fiery furnace, they would have never known the truth of Psalm 139: 7-10: that there is absolutely nowhere that we can go to escape the all-encompassing presence of God. Third, God's *no* allows him to glorify himself. Because God did not intervene in the manner that he could have, another miracle happened: a prideful king acknowledged the sovereignty of God (vv. 28-29).

RESPONDING TO NO

What should we do when God says *no*? Fundamentally, accepting what feels like a discouraging and disappointing response involves growing to a place in which what we want is synonymous with what God wants. As Christ submitted himself to the will of The Father (Luke 22: 42), and the Hebrew boys were steadfast in their commitment to God, independent of the outcome (Daniel 3: 16-18), can we say the same for ourselves? When we accept the best of times and the worst of times, our praise becomes authentic, consistent with Habakkuk 3: 17-18, and not contingent on anything but our love for who God is. Like Paul and Silas, when we offer meaningful praise to God despite being shackled in metaphorical prisons (Acts 16: 25-26), we demonstrate that our commitment to God far exceeds any tangible reward.

Friends, may our praise never be motivated only by what God can do for us, but rather the internalization of our love for him; knowing that a great God who says *no* has been, and will always be, deserving of great praise.

PERSONAL REFLECTION AND MEDITATION

1. Think of a situation in which God told you NO although you wanted him to say YES. What did you learn from this experience?

2. When God answers your prayers in ways that you think are unfair, what do you think he is teaching you?

Thank you for always having my best interest

at heart. Give me the strength to trust your no

as much as your yes. Amen.

SPRING, LENT
AND EASTER

IT'S A NEW SEASON!

For everything there is a season, a time for every activity under heaven.

Ecclesiastes 3: 1

At the risk of using a clichéd phrase, it's a new season! Really, it is. Spring has sprung and warmer days and increased hours of daylight consistently await us in the weeks and months ahead. But lest we overlook the spiritual significance of this [new] season, let's focus on what we can do to make the most of where we are in our personal histories with God while on our respective paths to spiritual maturity.

A TIME FOR EVERYTHING

Written by Pete Seeger and recorded by The Byrds, "To Everything There Is A Season (Turn! Turn! Turn!)" is a musical adaptation of Ecclesiastes 3 (vv. 1-8).[9] Attributed to King Solomon, the passage expresses the inevitability of change. As winter becomes spring, spring becomes summer, summer eventually becomes fall, and fall once again is the precursor to winter, our lives follow in similar fashion. In other words, if our present situations are not all that we desire them to be, we should be encouraged knowing that they won't always be this way. Financial struggles, health challenges, career stress, and in the words of Pastor Kevin Bond, "the vicissitudes of life's ever changing variables," did not come to stay. In fact, as we read throughout the scriptures, these things *came to pass.* Their season is temporary. The psalmist, in his 30th division, boldly declares it this way in verse 5: …*weeping may stay for the night, but rejoicing comes in the morning.* Because there is a time for everything, better days are ahead.

But amidst the encouragement of all that is to come, do we know what we should be doing in this season of our lives? Is it time to plant? Or, is it time to reap? Is it time to speak up about various atrocities that plague our communities? Or, is it time to be silent? While it may be time to hold on to some things, perhaps it's time to discard the unnecessary elements that are hindering our continued growth in the things of God. Today, if we don't know, let's ask God and wait for him to answer us.

A TIME TO CLEAN

Naturally speaking, spring is symbolic of newness and growth. The cold, dark months of winter have been replaced with the warmth and light of a time that is ripe with possibilities. As it is in the natural, so it is in the spiritual; but we must be careful to prepare ourselves to receive all that God desires to bring to fruition.

In the ensuing weeks, some will find themselves engaging in spring cleaning as they tidy their basements, attics, and garages; but what about embarking upon a spiritual spring cleaning? In other words, to position ourselves to fully benefit from what God is doing now, some of the habits (e.g., ways of thinking) that were present in the past no longer have a place in our lives. And as we prayerfully consider the adjustments that are necessary for us, we should remember that small and seemingly insignificant changes can have profound impact. For example, when God created the world in Genesis 1, one of the first things he did was establish order in a universe that was without form (v. 2). These words are recorded in verse 6: *"...Let there be a space between the waters to separate the waters of the heavens from the waters of the earth."*

Having been made in the image of God (v. 26), we are charged to operate as he does—in order, rather than chaos and confusion—and sometimes the best way to do this is by removing the clutter from our lives. While these things may not necessarily be bad or wrong, they also may not add any value as it relates to the plan, purpose, and will of God for our lives. In other words, let's get organized! Let's align our priorities to be consistent with God's word. Perhaps most importantly, let's remove the distractions that hinder us from clearly hearing the voice of the Lord.

A TIME TO REFOCUS

Although the first quarter of the year will soon be a memory, it is not too late to recommit ourselves to achieving what we were excited about only a few months ago.

As springing forward is associated with this season, let's allow the natural momentum to propel us into a new spiritual season. Because there is a time for everything, what is it time for us to do? What needs to be cleaned up and organized in our lives? And, how will we ensure that we are more focused than ever to fulfill the Lord's perfect plan for our lives?

PERSONAL REFLECTION AND MEDITATION

1. As you consider your life's purpose and the goals that you want to accomplish, what needs to be cleaned up or reorganized in your life?

2. What specific steps can you take to restructure your life so that you are moving closer to accomplishing your goals?

3. At this moment in time, do you know what you should be doing? If so, are you doing those things? Are there areas in which you can improve? If so, what are they and how can you improve?

4. If you are not doing what you should be doing, what specific steps can you take so that you are doing what God expects of you in this season of your life?

Thank you for the seasons as they remind me that better days are ahead. Help me to make the most of every season. Amen.

LENTEN MEDITATION: MORE OF GOD AND LESS OF ME

But the Holy Spirit produces this kind of fruit in our lives: love, joy, peace, patience, kindness, goodness, faithfulness, gentleness, and self-control...

Galatians 5: 22-23

Although the Lenten Season is upon us, I won't ask you to give up anything for 40 days. Instead, I challenge you to consider what you will take on, not for 40 days, but for the rest of your life. Through the lens of The Fruit of The Spirit, how can we use these 40 days of preparation as an opportunity to be more intentional about displaying these attributes in our lives?

THE FRUIT OF THE SPIRIT IS LOVE

Contextually, Paul is referencing agape love or love that is selfless, sacrificial, and unconditional. To illustrate this idea, Romans 5: 8 is perhaps the greatest example: *But God showed his great love for us by sending Christ to die for us while we were still sinners.* In other words, as there was nothing that we did to earn God's love, there is nothing that we can do to stop God from loving us (Romans 8: 38-39). Unlike the ways of the world, Christ instructs and expects us to love all people—including our enemies (Matthew 5: 43-48).

So, what's the lesson? We have not loved until we love those who do not, and perhaps never will, love us in return. Though a sobering truth, may this Lenten Season be the beginning of the display of agape love—true love that seeks nothing in return.

THE FRUIT OF THE SPIRIT IS JOY

Philippians 4: 11 and 12: *...for I have learned how to be content with whatever I have. I know how to live on almost nothing or with everything. I have learned the secret of living in every situation, whether it is with a full stomach or empty, with plenty or little.* Although we've certainly heard it before, it's worth sharing again: joy and happiness are not synonymous. Whereas happiness is often predicated on our temporary, tangible comforts, joy transcends our present state and position in life. Joy is the embodiment of Paul and Silas' midnight praise despite being wrongfully imprisoned in a Philippian jail (Acts 16: 23-26) and the commitment of worshippers to give God what he is due regardless of what is happening in and around our lives (Habakkuk 3: 17-18).

Even if it has not been our practice, may these 40 days signal the beginning of a life that is fully content in the God of our salvation—knowing that he who holds the uncertainties of tomorrow also holds our hands.

THE FRUIT OF THE SPIRIT IS PEACE

Peace, in this context, is more than the absence of strife or tension. Amongst other things, peace also involves reconciliation. Peace, therefore, is active (Matthew 5: 9; Hebrews 12: 14).

Rather than simply avoiding conflict in the name of peace, let us become peace agents—those who purposefully and intentionally pursue peace in our homes, communities, and houses of worship.

THE FRUIT OF THE SPIRIT IS PATIENCE

Similar to other aspects of The Fruit, patience is centered on our reactions to others—especially when they offend us or do things that are unfair and unjust. Instead of responding in ways that are justifiable by our human emotions, growing to consistently display this element of our Christian character leads us to respond to our fellow man in the same manner that God responds to us: by being compassionate, gracious, slow to anger, and abounding in love (Psalm 103: 8).

THE FRUIT OF THE SPIRIT IS KINDNESS

Although I don't know who originally coined this phrase, many of us have likely seen or heard it: *Say what you mean but don't say it mean.* Selah.

THE FRUIT OF THE SPIRIT IS GOODNESS

Do we have a benevolent spirit? Do we seek to do good to those who are unable to do so for themselves? Are we moved to serve the least of these according to Matthew 25: 31-46?

THE FRUIT OF THE SPIRIT IS FAITHFULNESS

As followers of Christ, we should be dependable. When we commit ourselves to various activities, we should see them to completion. Are we men and women of integrity? Or, do we require reminders to fulfill our responsibilities? Regardless of what the past has been, today is a new day that offers the opportunity to do better and to be better by the grace of Almighty God.

THE FRUIT OF THE SPIRIT IS GENTLENESS

Because of the culture in which we live, humility is often perceived as weakness rather than strength. Especially for men, needing the assistance of others is erroneously associated with less than flattering connotations. As a teenager, the best advice in this area came from my pastor and mentor, Bishop Roderick Caesar, Jr.: *Be teachable.* Not only do humble people depend on the Lord (Proverbs 3: 5-6), but they also surround themselves with a multitude of counselors (Proverbs 11: 14). Throughout this Lenten Season, perhaps we should consider how our views of humility might need to be revised in light of the character of Christ.

THE FRUIT OF THE SPIRIT IS SELF-CONTROL

In many ways, life, especially the Christian life, is about developing self-control—the ability to master our desires and passions rather than these things mastering us. To borrow a psychological term, delayed gratification refers to an individual's ability to defer pleasure in order to obtain something, usually of greater value, that he or she ultimately desires. As we are enticed by distractions during this Lenten Season, let's delay gratification. Specifically, let's learn to view the way of escape (1 Corinthians 10: 13) for what it really is—a window of opportunity that we must crawl through, rather than a gaping door that will always be available.

PERSONAL REFLECTION AND MEDITATION

1. How can you be more loving?

2. How can you demonstrate more joy?

3. How can you be an agent of peace?

4. How can you be more patient with God and with others?

5. How can you be increasingly kind to others?

6. Through the lens of Matthew 25: 31-46, how can you demonstrate the love of Christ to others by being more benevolent?

7. How can you be a person of integrity by consistently following through on your commitments?

8. How can you be teachable and exercise humility?

9. How can you exercise more self-control?

Thank you for never giving me more than I can handle. Help me to see challenging situations in my life as opportunities to develop my Christian character. By your grace, help me to be more loving and to demonstrate more joy. Help me to be an agent of peace and to be more patient with you and with others. Give me the strength to be kind and benevolent to others, especially those who have been marginalized by systemic injustice. Thank you for helping me to be humble and to exercise self-control.

Amen.

A LENTEN MEDITATION:
I NEED MORE OF YOU

Have mercy on me, O God, because of your unfailing love. Because of your great compassion, blot out the stain of my sins... Purify me from my sins, and I will be clean; wash me, and I will be whiter than snow... Create in me a clean heart, O God. Renew a loyal spirit within me.

Psalm 51: 1, 7, 10

Each Ash Wednesday, people all over the world embark upon a 40-day spiritual journey of self-sacrifice that culminates on Resurrection Sunday. Seemingly ritualistic, this time of year typically includes abstaining from guilty pleasures. But more than avoiding the indulgences of chocolate, red meat, caffeine, social media, or our favorite television shows, the Lenten Season should be centered on the individual's commitment to drawing nearer to the person of Jesus Christ. In looking closer at Psalm 51 (vv. 1-15), there are 3 simple truths that can help place this season in proper perspective.

I NEED MORE THAN FORGIVENESS OF SIN

Written by David in response to his adulterous sin, Psalm 51 is one of the most familiar prayers recorded in scripture. Beginning with a focus on forgiveness, David's principal message is, *Lord, I'm sorry* (vv. 1-7) before he shifts his attention to restoration and purification (vv. 8-12). The benefit of reading this passage is that we are voyeurs into the intimate, personal, and private thoughts of a man—in spite of his imperfections—who is described as being *after God's own heart* (1 Samuel 13: 14). Through all of his misfortunes, mishaps, missteps, and mistakes, David's desire to be close to God remained central to his existence. And it was this closeness that enabled David to experience the conviction of his sin, which made him uncomfortable until he sought the mercy of God. Forgiveness, however, was not enough. For David, I'm sorry was just the beginning.

I NEED TO BE MADE ANEW

In verses 8 through 12 David concentrates on what should happen after we seek forgiveness: I need to do things differently by being made anew. Such a cry characterizes true repentance—a sincere turning away from sin and changing of the mind. But lest we overlook a profound theological truth, let's consider verse 10 (English Standard Version): *Create in me a pure heart, O God, and renew a right spirit within me.* Of all the Hebrew words for create, *Bara,* which is used in the original text, is particularly significant because it is the only one that implies God as the subject. In other words, it is God who creates. It is God who makes all things new. But not only does God create, but he also creates from nothing! Used in Genesis 1: 1, he who made the world from nothing can fashion something new and beautifully meaningful from the chaos, confusion, and complications of our sinful lives.

NOW WHAT?

Verses 13 through 15: *Then I will teach your ways to rebels, and they will return to you. Forgive me for shedding blood, O God who saves; then I will joyfully sing of your forgiveness. Unseal my lips, O Lord, that my mouth may praise you.* After David confesses his sins, asks to be restored and made anew, his response to God is not only of worship and praise but also service (ministry) to others. In other words, his experiences were not meant to make him miserable, but they served as a catalyst for change within his own life and subsequently the lives of others.

As Matthew 4: 1-11 serves as the Biblical precedent for the contemporary observance of the Lenten Season, it also prepared Christ for his three-year miraculous and life changing ministry. Similar to David's prayer, the significance of Christ's spiritual journey was not that he abstained from food and water, but rather because he took on other things by spending quality time with God. Specifically, he was praying and fasting. Symbolically, whereas fasting might be likened unto not doing certain things, praying might be viewed as actively talking to God and drawing closer to him. Both were necessary. Behavioral psychologists might say it this way: in order to change an unhealthy behavior, it is not enough to simply stop doing it; we must also develop an appropriate replacement behavior to take its place.

So friends, what is Lent really about? Romans 12: 1-2:

> *And so, dear brothers and sisters, I plead with you to give your bodies to God because of all he has done for you. Let them be a living and holy sacrifice—the kind he will find acceptable. This is truly the way to worship him. Don't copy the behavior and customs of this world, but let God transform you into a new person by changing the way you think...*

Offering our total selves to God is only possible by having a renewed mind that thinks differently about what we do. In other words, if we no longer want to sin, we must learn to think differently about sin.

More than temporary abstinence, let's remember that this 40-day spiritual journey is about being changed from the inside out by the continual renewing of our minds.

PERSONAL REFLECTION AND MEDITATION

1. During the Lenten Season, what specific qualities of Christ (see Galatians 5: 22-23) can you take on to become more like him?

2. When the Lenten Season ends, how can you continue becoming more like Christ?

---•●•---

Thank you for placing within me the desire to be more like you. Help me to focus more on growing closer to you than temporarily abstaining from some of my favorite things. Give me the grace and strength to always spend quality time with you so that I will continue to grow in the grace and knowledge of Jesus Christ. Amen.

---•●•---

DON'T FORGET TO REMEMBER: YOU ARE ALWAYS ON HIS MIND

For all the pain, suffering, agony, and shame recorded by Isaiah, the Gospels let us know that we were on his mind. He was beaten so that ultimately we could have access to not only physical healing, but more importantly to the ultimate spiritual healing that is found in freedom from the bondage of sin.

A complete and accurate understanding of the Word of God is invaluable. One of the best ways to develop such an understanding is to seek the parallel connections between the Old and New Testaments. As the Gospels written by Matthew, Mark, Luke, and John are not islands unto themselves, in the same manner, the Old and New Testaments are complementary. As we pause to remember the sacrifice of Good Friday, which was a necessary precursor to the victory of Resurrection Sunday, let's briefly consider Isaiah 53.

The 12 verses of Isaiah 53 are centered on the person and event that are the fundamentals of our faith: Jesus Christ and the crucifixion. Lest we become desensitized to the anguish experienced by Christ on the cross at the expense of artistic renderings of this pivotal moment in history, Isaiah provides several vivid illustrations. In verse 3 he reminds us of his emotional burden: *He was despised and rejected—a man of sorrows, acquainted with deepest grief...* To remind us of the physical pain he endured, these words are recorded in verse 4: *Yet it was our weaknesses he carried; it was our sorrows that weighed him down. And we thought his troubles were a punishment from God, a punishment for his own sins!* Verse 5 is arguably the most familiar of the passage: *But he was pierced for our rebellion, crushed for our sins. He was beaten so we could be whole. He was whipped so we could be healed.* As an appropriate summation, the chapter ends with these words: *...he exposed himself to death... He bore the sins of many...*

But as we remember all that Christ endured upon the cross, we should also consider two questions. First, why would he subject himself to such pain? Next, what held him to the cross? Friends, it wasn't the nails that held Jesus to the cross. Although Isaiah wrote in the Old Testament about the Suffering Servant, the revelatory insight about why he remained hanging upon the tree is found in the Gospels as they recount what is commonly referred to as the *Seven Last Words* or *Cries From The Cross*. Quickly, let's consider the first three…

FATHER, FORGIVE THEM, FOR THEY DON'T KNOW WHAT THEY ARE DOING: LUKE 23: 34

Even while hanging on the cross and enduring excruciating pain, Jesus wasn't too busy to extend grace and mercy to those by whose hands he was being terribly mistreated.

I ASSURE YOU, TODAY YOU WILL BE WITH ME IN PARADISE: LUKE 23: 43

These words were spoken by Jesus to one of the guilty criminals who hung on the cross next to him. While one of the thieves mocked Jesus along with the crowd, the other's heart had been changed. Despite life slowly leaving his body, Jesus wasn't too pre-occupied to offer the gift of salvation. Because it is never too late, even in his final hour, the savior's arms remained outstretched to welcome all who would believe and receive.

DEAR WOMAN, HERE IS YOUR SON… HERE IS YOUR MOTHER: JOHN 19: 26 & 27

Another illustration of why Christ remained on the cross can be understood through the humanistic perspective. Although he was 100% God, at the same time he was 100% man. And because of his humanity, Christ was concerned with the feelings of those he loved: specifically his mother and beloved disciple, John. Jesus, though near to death, wasn't too busy to offer consolation and comfort to his mother and friend.

What, then, is the connection between the Old Testament prophetic words of Isaiah and the New Testament Gospel accounts of Jesus' words on the cross? For all the pain, suffering, agony, and shame recorded by Isaiah, the Gospels let us know that we were on his mind. He was beaten so that ultimately we could have access to not only physical healing, but more importantly to the ultimate spiritual healing that is found in freedom from the bondage of sin (1 Peter 2: 24). Just like those at Calvary who did not recognize the gravity of their sin, often times neither do we. But the savior was still forgiving and still saving—even until his very last moments. And as the quintessential son and faithful friend, some of Christ's final thoughts were centered on the well-being of Mary and John. Always loving and always giving, he was never consumed by his own pain.

So although we anticipate a glorious celebration of victory on Resurrection Sunday, let us not forget to remember the ultimate sacrifice of Good Friday when more than 2000 years ago, and still today, you and I were on his mind.

PERSONAL REFLECTION AND MEDITATION

1. Use this space to write your thoughts and reflections on this essay.

2. What was especially meaningful to you?

YES, JESUS LOVES ME

But God showed his great love for us by sending Christ to die for us while we were still sinners.

Romans 5: 8

Released in 1997, Kirk Franklin's "Love" masterfully combines a haunting melody with equally powerful lyrics: *Love, a word that comes and goes, but few people really know what it means to really love somebody...*[10] In trying to capture the essence of God's love, these words are also included: *...I'm so glad your love will stay, 'cause I love you; and you show me, Jesus, what it really means to love...* One of the most moving sections of the piece follows a climactic crescendo and conveys this fundamental quality of God's love: *...When I should have died you loved me, I'll never know why you loved me; it's a mystery to me now I'm glad I see Jesus. When all hope was gone you loved me... now I can go on 'cause you love me...* Without discounting Franklin's contribution to the canon of Gospel songs about love, William Batchelder Bradbury provided melodic structure to Anna Bartlett Warner's poem "Jesus Loves Me" more than 150 years ago.[11] In fact, Bradbury added the famous refrain: *Yes, Jesus loves me. Yes, Jesus loves me. Yes, Jesus loves me. The Bible tells me so.*

As we approach Resurrection Sunday, defensibly the most significant event on the Christian calendar, how do we know that God loves us? According to Bradbury, *The Bible tells [us] so.* Friends, what does the Bible say about God's love for you and me?

GOD LOVED US WHEN WE DID NOT, AND PERHAPS NEVER WOULD, LOVE HIM IN RETURN

Romans 5: 8: *But God showed his great love for us by sending Christ to die for us while we were still sinners.* In this verse, the profundity of God's love is captured in a single word: while. Said another way, *at the same time* or *during the time when* we were not thinking about God, he sent his son to die for our sins. And because Christ died, we can live forever. Rather than waiting for us to show that we were interested in a relationship with him, God proved his unconditional commitment to us in the most unselfish of ways.

GOD LOVED US WITH EVERYTHING THAT HE HAD

More than God's love not being contingent on our love for him, it was also sacrificial. John 3: 16—*"For this is how God loved the world: He gave his one and only Son, so that everyone who believes in him will not perish but have eternal life.* Consider this: beyond what Christ experienced while dying on the cross, the crucifixion was also excruciatingly painful for God, The Father. Because he had no other sons, sending Jesus was sending all—literally everything—he had.

CHRIST LOVED US BY TAKING ON A DEBT WITHOUT THE EXPECTATION OF REPAYMENT

Was it necessary for Christ to die? Was this the only way to satisfy the debt that was brought on by our sinful state? The answer is found in Hebrews 9: 22 (New International Version): *In fact, the law requires that nearly everything be cleansed with blood, and without the shedding of blood there is no forgiveness.* This principle was repeatedly illustrated throughout the Old Testament whenever an animal was sacrificed to atone for sin (Leviticus 16: 3, 5-6, 11, 20-22). But because of Christ, the once-and-for-all sacrificial lamb who took on the penalty without complaint (Isaiah 53: 7), this is no longer necessary. We know that Christ loves us because he accepted the responsibility for what he did not do (Isaiah 53: 4, 12) by paying the ultimate price for charges that he did not incur. And like God's love in Romans 5: 8, Christ did this without expecting anything in return.

CHRIST LOVES US BECAUSE HE REFUSES TO LEAVE US IN OUR CURRENT SITUATIONS

John 3: 17: *God sent his Son into the world not to judge the world, but to save the world through him.* While salvation is the foundation upon which a full and rewarding life that is spent in perpetual fellowship and relationship with God rests, this is only the beginning of our Christian experience. In other words, while a personal relationship with Christ does not always instantaneously erase the reality of conditions with which we struggle, it underscores our continual dependence on him to help us overcome every situation and become better than we were the day before. So because God loves us, he allows us to experience various challenges and circumstances to ultimately develop our Christian character (Galatians 5: 22-23; James 1: 2-4). Yes, God loves us just the way we are; but he also loves us too much to allow us to stay the way we are.

DO WE LOVE LIKE JESUS?

Although God is sovereign, he is neither a dictator nor a tyrant. Therefore, when we are faced with decisions, He allows us to choose what we want to do (Joshua 24: 15; Revelation 3: 20). God's love that was expressed by sending his only son to die for our sins, and Christ's obedient response to the will of The Father (Luke 22: 42), were conscious decisions and the epitome and embodiment of unconditional love.

When Jesus says, *"Father forgive them, for they do not know what they are doing..."* (Luke 23: 34; New International Version), he is praying for those who were actively killing him. Moreover, God used Paul, who was once an enemy of The Church (1 Corinthians 15: 9; Galatians 1: 13) and who struggled with an unnamed besetting sin (2 Corinthians 12: 7-10), to write most of the New Testament and help Christians (even today) grow in the grace and knowledge of Jesus Christ. So if Christ spent some of his final moments praying for the forgiveness of those who were killing him, and Paul became one of the greatest messengers for God despite his past persecution of Christians (Galatians 1: 15), rest assured that God forgives and loves you, too.

Bob Sorge, in his book, *Exploring Worship: A Practical Guide to Praise and Worship,* discusses a concept known as the Horizontal Function of Praise.[12] Essentially, while praise is a vertical interaction between God and man, there are horizontal benefits for those in our company (Acts 16: 25-34). In the spirit of Sorge, what is the horizontal function of love? Having been beneficiaries of God's love, how does this impact those whom we encounter each day? Because love is a sacrificial and conscious decision that is not dependent on the actions of others, do we love like Jesus?

PERSONAL REFLECTION AND MEDITATION

1. Think about the manner in which Christ loves you. What are some words or feelings that describe his love for you?

2. What are some of the most challenging aspects that prevent you from loving like Jesus?

3. How can you learn to love others like Jesus loves you?

Thank you for loving me unconditionally. Despite my shortcomings, help to receive your love. By your grace, help me to love others like you have loved me. Amen.

ENCOURAGEMENT

MY GRACE IS SUFFICIENT: BLACK, CHRISTIAN, AND LIVING WITH MENTAL ILLNESS

Can I be saved and depressed? Can I be saved and have an anxiety disorder? Can I be saved and live with mental illness?

Life will not always be easy. Even while enjoying the peace of a personal relationship with Christ, we are fraught with the myriad challenges of the human condition. For a variety of reasons, it is necessary to focus on a very real, yet less talked about subject within the African American faith community. Although we have become increasingly open to discussing and effectively addressing the realities of mental illness impacting those in our families, churches and neighborhoods, let's look closer...

A CONDITION THAT WE DID NOT CHOOSE

Having been reared in the African American classical Pentecostal tradition, there seemed to be an unspoken, but sometimes spoken, devaluation of mental illness. Even more concerning and insensitive was the inappropriate use of scripture to justify these ideas. For example, because we should be *anxious for nothing* (Philippians 4: 6; New King James Version), anxiety, therefore, was [subjectively judged to be] "not of God." Albeit subtle, this assertion, coupled with God wanting us to have *life more abundantly* (John 10:10; King James Version), which was erroneously interpreted as the happy life, inadvertently degraded those experiencing the reality of being Christian, yet living with mental illness.

As a people who have historically held its faith in high regard, it has been especially challenging to effectively address mental illness within the African American community. Rather than being encouraged to participate in counseling or therapy with a qualified professional, African Americans have often been admonished to pray about their circumstances. As a result, many have asked themselves: Can I be saved and depressed? Can I be saved and have an anxiety disorder? Can I be saved and live with mental illness?

Through my personal growth process, I have realized that the answer to these questions is yes. If Christians can have cancer, diabetes, and hypertension, we can certainly have anxiety, depression, and a host of other mental illnesses. Moreover, while some experience the aforementioned maladies as a consequence of their choices (e.g., poor diet and limited exercise), others were born with these potentially debilitating diseases. The same holds true for mental illness: many are faced with managing the life-long course of a condition that stems from biological and genetic factors. And what about those who were victims of various types of abuse and trauma that affected their mental health? Regardless of what has led to your mental illness, be encouraged because you have been fearfully and wonderfully made (Psalm 139: 14) in the image of God (Genesis 1: 27) and nothing—not even mental illness—can separate you from his love (Romans 8: 39).

SOCIETAL PERCEPTIONS OF WEAKNESS

Several years ago, I was working with a male high school student who was experiencing significant mental health difficulty. His father, however, felt strongly that his son's condition was less serious than it was, and he instead needed to *man up*. For an impressionable adolescent who was particularly sensitive to his father's acceptance and approval, effective treatment necessarily entailed reshaping the father's perspective on mental health. Like this youngster, men (and women) who are living with mental illness need to know that they are not weak— a word that is almost always associated with negative connotations— but they're human.

Unlike women, men are less likely to verbalize their feelings. Coupled with the fallacious thinking that mental illness is synonymous with, or even caused by weakness, this helps to explain why men don't always seek the professional care that they need. For these reasons, it is incumbent upon churches and communities to create safe spaces in which men can express their innermost emotions. In the same manner that schools are often the point of access for a variety of services for children and families, it is more than appropriate for religious institutions to adopt a full service model and provide the much-needed supports to meet the spiritual, physical, social, emotional, and mental health needs of its parishioners and surrounding community.

MY GRACE IS SUFFICIENT

Why me? Is God punishing me? Is my mental illness a consequence of sin? Why was I made this way? Why did God allow this to happen to me? Why doesn't God take this away from me? For African American Christians living with mental illness, these are likely some of their most pressing questions. While I don't have all of the answers to these questions, I find comfort and strength in 2 Corinthians 12: 7-10.

Written by the Apostle Paul, these verses juxtapose humanity with spiritual maturity. Although we do not know (and ultimately it's not important) the specifics of Paul's thorn in the flesh, we can be sure that it was inconvenient. Uncomfortable. Painful. It was a distraction designed to discourage Paul from fulfilling his purpose; and although he prayed, and prayed, and prayed for the Lord to remove this nuisance from him, the answer was no (see *When God Says No,* p. 57). But more importantly, the Lord's response also included what He would do instead. Although I am not going to remove this difficult and seem-ingly impossible situation from you, my grace is sufficient—it's enough—for you. Although you want this terrible thing to be taken away from you, what you really need is my grace—supernatural strength to endure.

Friends, have you considered that your mental illness could be your thorn in the flesh—something that the Lord will not remove, but whose grace is strong enough to sustain you? Like Paul, God doesn't always take away our incon-veniences because he is developing our Christian character (Galatians 5:22-23). And as we are accomplishing great things for God, the thorn in the flesh reminds us that he is the one who chose us: not because we are perfect, but because he can use anyone because he is perfect.

PERSONAL REFLECTION AND MEDITATION

1. Use this space to write your thoughts and reflections on this essay.

2. What was especially meaningful to you?

3. If you are living with mental illness, what has this taught you about God and your relationship with God?

4. If you had the opportunity, what would you like your friends, family, co-workers, neighbors, and other Christians to know about living with mental illness?

---•●•---

Thank you that I have been fearfully and wonderfully made. Thank you that nothing can separate me from your love. Thank you that your grace is enough to sustain me through everything that comes my way. Amen.

---•●•---

TO ENCOURAGE YOU: THE PROPER PERSPECTIVE ON GOING THROUGH

Our steps have been divinely orchestrated by a loving
God who always has our best interest at heart.

Nothing just happens. Yes, some things are beyond our control; but nothing just happens. Because there is a time for everything (Ecclesiastes 3: 1), all that we have done, all that we are doing now, and all that we will do in the future fits into God's purpose and plan for our lives. Be encouraged. Our steps have been divinely orchestrated by a loving God who always has our best interest at heart (Psalm 37: 23-24; Jeremiah 29: 11).

THE IMPORTANCE OF PERSPECTIVE

Perspective—the manner in which we think about our lives and our circumstances—significantly influences how we go through challenging situations. For this reason, we must align our thoughts with God's thoughts (1 Corinthians 2: 16). Regardless of what we are going through, are we viewing things from a God perspective rather than an understandable, yet selfish, human point of view? While it does not change the reality of going through, it helps to know that there is purpose in going through.

YOU DID NOTHING WRONG

One of the most common responses to going through is to immediately ask ourselves: What did I do to deserve this? While facing various challenges, we assume that we are being punished for our wrongdoing. This, however, is not always true, especially because God does not do things like we do (Isaiah 55: 8-9) or respond to us based on our shortcomings (Psalm 103: 8-13). Therefore, going through is not always synonymous with receiving a celestial scolding. One of the best illustrations of this principle is through the life of Job, a man who did nothing wrong (Job 1: 1, 8) yet he experienced significant hardship (Job 1: 13-19; 2: 7).

Because going through is not necessarily punitive, we should consider it a privilege when we experience various difficulties because they exist to make us better (James 1: 2-4). In fact, the mechanism by which the Lord develops our Christian character (i.e., The Fruit of The Spirit; Galatians 5: 22-23) is by allowing us to endure uncomfortable and difficult seasons. In other words, to grow in kindness, he places us in situations in which we must practice being kind to others. To become more patient, he gives us opportunities to exercise patience—perhaps through marriage or raising children. To be more loving, God purposely places us in the company of those who are not easy to love so that we would learn to demonstrate the sacrificial and unconditional love of Christ. And here's the best part: God is so committed to developing each aspect of our Christian character that he gives us ample opportunity to grow until we have been fully perfected!

So the next time you're going through, rather than assuming you did something wrong (because you probably didn't), consider the aspect of your Christian character that God is perfecting.

YOU CAN HANDLE THIS

Also noteworthy from Job is that God carefully chooses who will go through (Job 1: 8; 2: 3). And because nothing catches God by surprise, not only does he choose who will go through, he also places limits on what we will go through (Job 1: 12; 2: 6). In other words, because he loves us and knows us, God will never give us more than we can handle (1 Corinthians 10: 13).

So as difficult as it seems today, you will get through this. Although you feel that you can't, you've felt that way before and you're still standing. And not only are you still standing, you're stronger, wiser, and better than you've ever been! Friends, the next time you're going through, be encouraged. Like Job, God has chosen you because you can handle it!

IT'S NOT ABOUT YOU

John's account of Jesus traveling from Judea to Galilee (John 4: 3) contains a seemingly insignificant detail in verse 4: *He had to go through Samaria on the way.* In other words, although Samaria was not his final destination, he had to go through it to ultimately get to where he was going. And so it is with us today: the temporary circumstances in which we find ourselves are simply part of the journey to reach our predestined destination.

Consider this: going through Samaria had less to do with Jesus than who he met while at the well: a Samaritan woman—someone with whom he was not allowed to interact based on Jewish law (vv. 9, 27). But because Jesus has always been focused on changing people's lives, he defied tradition and engaged in a meaningful conversation with the woman that changed her life (vv. 7-29). In light of this, what would have happened if Jesus didn't go through Samaria? Well, the woman would have missed a divine encounter with the source of her total fulfillment, rather than the temporary satisfaction that came from physical water and her many failed relationships (vv. 13-18). So if Jesus didn't go through Samaria, it wasn't that he would have missed anything; but the woman—the one who needed him to be in that place at that time—would have missed a once in a lifetime opportunity to be in his presence and receive all that she needed.

Like the woman needed to meet Jesus as he was going through, there are people who need to meet you as you're going through. So rather than complaining about how difficult things may be, change your perspective. Think about those whom the Lord has purposely placed in your path. Think about how you can positively impact someone's life. Because your steps are ordered, know that where you are is exactly where God wants you to be. Although it's not your final destination, God has placed you there for a reason; not only for you, but those whom you will encounter as you're going through.

PERSONAL REFLECTION AND MEDITATION

1. Ask the Lord to show you what he wants you to learn (about him and yourself) as you are going through challenging situations.

2. How can you change your perspective when going through difficult circumstances?

3. Despite being inconvenient and uncomfortable, how does serving others change your perspective on going through?

———◀)•●•(▶———

Thank you for always teaching me through every situation I experience. Thank you that going through won't last forever. Help me to grow from my moments of discomfort and to help others in the process. Amen.

———◀)•●•(▶———

TO ENCOURAGE YOU: THE OTHER SIDE OF THROUGH

For our present troubles are small and won't last very long...

2 Corinthians 4: 17

Be encouraged. There is more to life than going through.

DIFFERENT PERSPECTIVES

As individuals, we have different backgrounds and life experiences. However, despite our diversity, God is committed to meeting each of us at the point of our need and revealing things to us in ways that are relevant and meaningful. For this reason, the New Testament Gospels often recount the same events from various perspectives. As each record accentuates a point of view that would have otherwise been lost in a single retelling, reading each account provides the most comprehensive understanding of what actually happened.

Recorded in Matthew (8: 23-27), Mark (4: 35-41), and Luke (8: 22-25), the disciples encountered a storm while travelling from Galilee to the *other side*. As the winds were blowing and they feared for their lives, Matthew writes, *Lord, save us! We're going to drown (verse 25)!* Similarly, Luke records these words: *Master, Master, we're going to drown (verse 24)!* The retelling that is captured in Mark, however, is markedly different. Although each writer depicted the disciples as men who were desperate for divine intervention, Mark suggests that they were also slightly annoyed with Jesus as they said, *Teacher, don't you care that we're going to drown (verse 38)?* Whereas Matthew and Luke focused on what they wanted Jesus to do, Mark questioned Jesus. Whereas the cries recorded by Matthew and Luke assumed that Jesus could save them, Mark wasn't necessarily doubting his ability to rescue them from the perils of the storm, but rather whether he cared enough to do so. In other words, I know that you can, but will you do this for me?

A CRISIS OF FAITH

Despite the differing, but not conflicting perspectives, the response from Jesus was the same and showed that the disciples were experiencing a crisis of faith (Matthew 8: 26-27; Mark 4: 40-41; Luke 8: 25). Like many of us, especially as we're going through storms of our own, the disciples were surprised that Jesus had everything under control. Despite walking and talking with him, and witnessing the many miracles he performed for others, when they needed Jesus to do something for them, their belief was clouded with unbelief (Mark 9: 24). Parenthetically, if others are critical of you because you're unsure of how you'll get through challenging situations, be encouraged. Faith and fear are not incompatible. More accurately, faith is the triumph over fear.

DIRECT EXPERIENCE

Although the miracles that Jesus had already performed showed unbelievers that he was the Son of God, they were also significant for the 12 men whom he called to help change the world. Moreover, because everything that we experience prepares us for what's coming next, the storm was not the end; but it was necessary so that the disciples could effectively minister to those on the other side. Even today, how can we encourage others to trust God through difficult seasons if we have not already trusted him for ourselves? How can we tell others to have faith in God if we have not overcome our uncertainty about what God will do for us? How we can tell others that God cares for them if we have not been convinced of this truth ourselves? After we've weathered storms with Jesus, and have personally experienced the supernatural power of God, nothing can challenge the reality of who God is.

THE OTHER SIDE OF THROUGH

As always, what we go through is never about us. Therefore, the significance of the storm is not that the disciples made it to the other side, but all that happened on the other side. In other words, the storm was less about the disciples than those whom they were destined to meet on the other side. In fact, not only did Jesus feed a crowd of more than 5,000 with a little boy's lunch (Mark 6: 33-44), but the same disciples who were amazed that he could handle the storm, also performed extraordinary deeds (Mark 6: 13). So not only does

Jesus have supernatural power, but because we know him, we too have the authority to positively affect those around us (John 14: 12).

2 Corinthians 4: 17: *For our present troubles are small and won't last very long...* As it was for the disciples, our present troubles are simply storms that we must go through. But here's the good news: storms are temporary. And although we might not realize it while we're going through, when we get to the other side, and meet people who need to experience the life changing love of God, we'll know that it was worth it.

PERSONAL REFLECTION AND MEDITATION

1. How has going through difficult situations strengthened aspects of your Christian character (Galatians 5: 22-23)? For example, how has going through helped you to become more patient?

2. How has going through difficult circumstances prepared you for what you are currently doing?

Thank you that going through difficult circumstances has purpose. Thank you for giving me opportunities to use my experiences to eventually help someone else. Help me to remember that you do all things well. Amen.

HAPPY
FATHER'S DAY

IN DEFENSE OF FATHERS

Please, for the sake of all men and fathers, be intentional about changing the narrative by operating from a position of strength: that most fathers willingly embrace their responsibility of what they have been called to be and do for their children.

Each year, on the third Sunday in June, men, women, boys, and girls throughout the United States celebrate Father's Day. If you are in a position to honor fathers, perhaps by planning a service or event at your respective house of worship, I encourage you to be intentional about making Father's Day different.

ENCOURAGE FATHERS

Although some might not readily admit it, on Mother's Day, women and mothers are celebrated and championed for being the wind beneath their children's wings along with other flowery sentiments. While this is certainly true, appropriate, and should never be understated, it is also an unfortunate truth that men are paid underhanded compliments as the sleeping giants who need to take their rightful places in their homes, churches, and communities. Please, for the sake of all men and fathers, do not do this. Rather than reminding men and fathers of all that they are not doing and all that they should become, celebrate them for their faithfulness to their families, churches, and communities. More than ties, socks, cologne, or tools, they will love and appreciate you for this.

NORMALIZE GOOD FATHERS AND FATHERHOOD

Contrary to popular opinion and sensationalized media accounts, most fathers, especially those in the African American community, are not deadbeat dads, but are committed to their children. In fact, data from a 2013 report published by the Centers for Disease Control and Prevention (CDC) showed that African American fathers are more actively involved in the lives of their children, as measured by a variety of indicators, than White or Latino fathers.[13] Coupled with the countless personal anecdotes that many have of their own father-heroes who were everything but ordinary, such data confirm that most fathers are not absent. Please, for the sake of all men and fathers, be intentional about changing the narrative by operating from a position of strength: that most fathers willingly embrace their responsibility of what they have been called to be and do for their children.

BE SENSITIVE

This next suggestion pertains not only to men and fathers, but all of God's children. Yes, it is true that most fathers are good fathers—providing for their children and being actively involved in their lives in meaningful ways. But as there are mothers who at times miss the mark, fathers, too, are imperfect. And the implications of this, even for adult children, are nonetheless significant. In fact, it can distort the manner in which people who genuinely love God ultimately view God. *How do I relate to God as a loving father when I never knew this from my earthly father? How do I associate unconditional love and acceptance with God when I never experienced this from a person who was supposed to show me these things?* While it might not be your story, these questions represent the reality for many in our families, congregations, and communities. And as the Body of Christ, we must be sensitive to the needs of one another. Therefore, pray for those who have strained relationships with their fathers. Pray for those who never knew the love of an earthly father. Pray for those who may be experiencing Father's Day without the man who loved them unconditionally and wholeheartedly. Pray, especially, for the children of John Crawford, III, Eric Garner, Alton Sterling, and countless other African American fathers gone too soon.

Last, be sensitive to fathers. Beneath their seemingly tough exteriors, fathers hurt; fathers cry; and fathers endure pain. As they shoulder the weight of providing for and protecting their families, they experience disappointments untold.

Perhaps these words found in Psalm 61 (vv. 1-3) might be a source of encouragement to the fathers in your midst: *O God, listen to my cry! Hear my prayer! From the ends of the earth, I cry to you for help when my heart is overwhelmed.*

Lead me to the towering rock of safety, for you are my safe refuge, a fortress where my enemies cannot reach me.

PERSONAL REFLECTION AND MEDITATION

1. How can you, your family, your community, and/or local faith community intentionally encourage fathers?

2. How can you, your family, your community, and/or local faith community intentionally normalize good fathers and fatherhood?

3. How can you, your family, your community, and/or local faith community be sensitive to those who, for a variety of reasons, are experiencing Father's Day without their fathers?

Thank you for our fathers. Help us to show them how much we love and appreciate them— not just today, but throughout the year. Amen.

IF YOU DON'T FATHER THEM, WHO WILL?

Fathers, do not provoke your children to anger by the way you treat them. Rather, bring them up with the discipline and instruction that comes from the Lord.

Ephesians 6: 4

When I was 14 or 15 years old, The Lord spoke to me: *If you don't go, who will?* At the time, I was preparing to speak to my peers about the importance of sharing the Gospel and the life of David seemed to be an appropriate illustration of this challenge. In 1 Samuel 17, when no one else was willing to fight Goliath (vv. 11, 24), David, a young shepherd-boy-musician, volunteered to face the uncircumcised Philistine (vv. 26-37). Rather than waiting for another, perhaps an older or more qualified soldier, David saw a need and answered the proverbial call. What would have happened if David wasn't willing to fight Goliath? How would history be different?

In the same manner, brothers, if we don't father the children entrusted to our care in our homes, churches, and communities, who will? As we approach the annual celebration that is dedicated to both fathers and father figures, let's take a few moments to consider this very important question. I especially want to encourage those who are not biological fathers but fathers, nonetheless.

FATHERS ACCEPT RESPONSIBILITY

First and foremost, men, especially fathers, accept responsibility. For those who have married women with children, this covenant necessarily includes a commitment to her children. As husbands to women with children, the manner in which we love and respect our wives, provide for our families, and lead them according to Biblical principles become daily examples to her children. Without

---

minimizing the significance of a child's biological father, men living in blended families must be careful to not discount their role and responsibilities. More than being physically present and financially dependable, are you emotionally available to the children in your home? Do they have your time and attention? Have you accepted the fatherly responsibilities of your blended family?

FATHERS ADJUST TO NEW EXPECTATIONS

Like other family systems, blended families have unique challenges. Whereas couples that marry without children might have the luxury of learning one another before juggling the added demands associated with raising a family, those in blended families must simultaneously adjust to a new marriage while negotiating all that comes with developing healthy, well-adjusted young people. Even when couples agree that they will always do whatever is in the best interest of the child, this is much easier said than done. What happens when what's in the best interest of the child is uncomfortable for me, as a man and as a husband? Without oversimplifying complex situations, men who love their wives and want the best for their children place their well-being above their own by genuinely adjusting to new expectations. Very importantly, this is not synonymous with lowering expectations; but for the sake of the children they love, fathers accept the awkwardness and inconveniences of their new normal—not passively or begrudgingly, but with a sincere spirit.

FATHERS ANSWER THE CALL

More than biology, fatherhood is about relationship. And not being a biological father does not lessen the important place that you have in a child's life. If you have been blessed to speak into the lives of young people and impact them in meaningful ways, in many respects, not only are you a father, but you also might be their only father figure. Therefore, if you don't father them, who will? If you don't teach them, who will? If you don't love them, who will? If you don't encourage them, who will?

Because children are impressionable and are carefully watching our actions, even when we least expect it, what will we do with such an amazing opportunity? It is my prayer that we would look to the words of the Apostle Paul recorded in the 4th verse of Ephesians 6 (Message Bible): *Fathers, don't exasperate your children by coming down hard on them. Take them by the hand and lead them in the way of the Master.*

Happy Father's Day.

PERSONAL REFLECTION AND MEDITATION

1. Are there children in your community or church who are living without a father or father figure? If so, prayerfully consider how you may be able to support their development. Speak to their mothers or guardians about your desire to support them and their children.

2. If you are struggling with the reality of living in a blended family, prayerfully consider how you can make the necessary adjustments. Share your feelings with your wife so that you can work through this situation together.

Thank you for the fathers and father figures
who love and support our children.   Bless
them for everything they do and for the many
sacrifices they make. Amen.

GOOD GOOD FATHER

You're a Good, Good Father; it's who you are, it's who you are, it's who you are.

Pat Barrett and Anthony Brown

Written by Pat Barrett and Anthony Brown, "**Good Good Father**" is an anthem that celebrates who God is and how he defines who we are.[14] Popularized by Contemporary Christian recording artist Chris Tomlin, this motif is echoed in a simple refrain: *You're a Good, Good Father; it's who you are, it's who you are, it's who you are. And I'm loved by you; it's who I am, it's who I am, it's who I am…* To honor the greatest man in my life, Rev. Stuart Barrett, Sr., I will highlight three ways in which he has been a good, good father to me.

HE TAUGHT ME THROUGH RELATIONSHIP

One of the most challenging aspects of working with people, especially young people, is the ability to develop a unique relationship with each one, without compromising the quality of these connections. Parenting multiple children is perhaps the best illustration of this idea. But because I don't have personal experience with this as a father, I will liken it unto a teacher's relationship with his students. Fundamentally, relationship is the foundation upon which learning occurs. Therefore, in order to effectively communicate information, first and foremost, teachers must establish meaningful connections with their students by consistently and intentionally investing the necessary effort to understand each one as an individual—their interests, moods, and idiosyncrasies—in order to know the manner in which instruction should be approached and delivered to achieve the greatest success.

My father, a former teacher, accomplished this masterfully. Although I didn't realize it as a child, it was clear to me as an adult. Like a good teacher, dad developed a unique relationship with each of my brothers and me—relationships that had a lot less to do with money and tangible items than what was most important: his time. Dad gave us his undivided attention. Not only was he physically present in our home, but he was emotionally available and invested in our individual lives and well-being.

One of the most important things my father did was to ensure that we spent more time with him as we were getting older. Having always served our local church, I remember it clearly: dad told us that he would be doing less [at church] because *you boys need me now.* Although I did not understand what this decision meant for the rest of my life, I am grateful for his wisdom and foresight. I fondly remember many Sunday afternoons that were spent sitting and talking around our dining room table. But not only did he talk to us, dad gave us a voice by listening to what we were saying. By listening, he understood how we were growing, and our thinking evolving—each in his own way.

The effort that my father spent developing individual relationships with each of us allowed him to support the dreams and endeavors that we found to be personally fulfilling. For one, it was taking him to the bowling alley or a music store to play drums. For another, it was sitting in the stands during his football games. For a third brother, it was cheering, loudly, at wrestling matches. For me, it was years spent paying for piano lessons and chauffeuring me to and from countless services and rehearsals. It was driving me to my college and graduate school interviews. Dad's ability to love individually, yet equally, taught me an invaluable lesson long before Gary Chapman's **New York Times Bestseller,** *The Five Love Languages: The Secret to Love that Lasts:* love is not about the manner in which we want to show people that we care; instead, it's about paying attention to what the object of our affection values so that we can love them in ways that are meaningful.[15] Because of his relationship with us, dad's love was demonstrated differently. In educational terms, it was differentiated and individualized so that each of us received exactly what we needed.

HE TAUGHT ME BY EXAMPLE

Because dad was an exceptional leader, he did so by example. In other words, he wasn't a *do as I say not as I do* type of father. Everything that he admonished us to do, and subsequently expected of us, was because he modeled these things.

I remember hearing him start the car early in the morning, sometimes six days each week. He would leave by 6:00 or 6:30 and not return until 6:00 in the evening. Although this seemed rather inconsequential at the time, it left an indelible impression on me. My father did what was necessary to provide for his family. I'm sure that some days were terribly cold. I'm sure that some days he simply did not feel like going to work. But despite these things, he showed us the importance of responsibility, hard work, and sacrifice.

For many years, my father was a worship leader. In fact, he was a large part of how I began playing in church more than 25 years ago. But before I understood the importance of musicians and singers being true to what they professed publicly, I lived with a father who led his family in prayer and praise. I can say a lot more about this, but suffice it to say that my father's life and example has had a profound impact on my appreciation of, and approach to, worship, praise, and music ministry.

Even in recent years, my father accomplished something that was nothing short of tremendous. Not wanting any of his grandchildren to have an excuse for not furthering their education, dad earned his Bachelor's and Master's degrees just shy of his 60th birthday. Dad's example showed us that nothing is impossible.

HE TAUGHT ME TO SERVE

Without exception, my father has taught me the most about serving others. A deacon for more than 15 years, those in his care often called upon my father when they needed help in various ways. Not being more than 12 years old, I remember my father leaving our home in Long Island to purchase and bring chicken to a family that lived more than 40 minutes away. I remember that it was a Saturday night. I remember that it was cold. I remember that it was late at night. These things, however, did not matter to my father. Someone was in need and he did all that he could to serve.

MY FATHER AND ME

As a school psychologist, I have the privilege of serving children, families, schools, and communities. And because of what he showed me, I make myself available to my students. Because he gave me a voice, I listen to young people so that they, too, will know that what they have to say is important.

I certainly did not realize how much my father was impacting me as I was growing up on Rutland Road. But now that I do, I'm grateful. I'm grateful that my father knows me. In fact, he told me that he knows me better than I know myself (smile). I had to have been in college when he said that he knew when I was home because the house felt differently. I liked hearing it then, and I still smile when I think about it now.

Because my brothers and I are now adults, dad says that his days of active parenting are over. Instead, he's a consultant parent: *you guys call me and I'll tell you what I think; but what you do is up to you.* Never too busy and always prepared with what I need, I am grateful for my father, my friend.

Happy Father's Day, Dad.

PERSONAL REFLECTION AND MEDITATION

1. How has God has been a good, good father to you?

2. If you're a father, how can you be a good, good father to your children?

Thank you for being a good good father to me.

Amen.

FREEDOM, PRIVILEGE AND JUSTICE

INDEPENDENCE DAY:
THE DAY HE SET ME FREE

…when did the Lord touch you? When did Jesus change your life?

Since 1776, the United States of America has celebrated its succession from England on the 4th day of July. With the signing and adoption of the Declaration of Independence, the once fledgling colonies secured their freedom as an independent nation, no longer subject to the authority of Great Britain. These words from would-be President John Adams to his wife Abigail seem to capture the excitement and gravity of the day:

> *… The second day of July 1776, will be the most memorable epoch in the history of America. I am apt to believe that it will be celebrated by succeeding generations as the great anniversary festival. It ought to be commemorated as the day of deliverance, by solemn acts of devotion to God Almighty. It ought to be solemnized with pomp and parade, with shows, games, sports, guns, bells, bonfires, and illuminations, from one end of this continent to the other, from this time forward forever more.*[16]

Although America's Independence Day is the 4th of July, more importantly, when is your personal Independence Day? So great was its freedom that fireworks, parades, and speeches commemorate this monumental occasion. Spiritually speaking, many would agree that the day when Christ liberated all of mankind by conquering sin, death, and the grave is a universal Christian Independence Day. But what about our personal Resurrection Days: the days that are scattered throughout the year and signify when Christ set us free?

No doubt, there are pivotal moments in our lives whose anniversaries are precisely annotated. For example, 1 Samuel 3 (vv. 1-10) recounts the Lord's calling of the young prophet. And because the events of that night were so personal and intimate, in my estimation, it would be virtually impossible for Samuel, even when he was much older, to forget how and when the Lord called him for his divine purpose. If he were asked, "How do you know that you're a prophet?" Samuel would likely respond with the utmost confidence by saying, "Because the Lord called me by my name." Moreover, even Jesus recognized when something meaningful happened in his life. While in the midst of a great multitude, he knew that someone touched him because there was a moment at which [healing] virtue left his body (Luke 8: 42-48). From both passages the lesson is simple: we should know when something significant happens in our lives. And even for the changes that manifest *as we go* (Luke 17: 14), because the leper returned to say thank you, he knew that he received his miracle from Jesus (Luke 17: 15-16).

As certain days are etched into our memories and are met with cards, flowers, gifts, and a host of other activities to celebrate their significance, in the same manner, when did the Lord touch you? When did Jesus change your life?

Friends, when is your Independence Day? If you don't have one, pick a day, perhaps today, and celebrate it forever.

PERSONAL REFLECTION AND MEDITATION

1. When do you celebrate your personal Independence Day?

2. How will you celebrate the day that Jesus set you free?

Thank you for setting me free. Amen.

ON FREEDOM, PRIVILEGE, AND JUSTICE

… When someone has been given much, much will be required in return; and when someone has been entrusted with much, even more will be required.

Luke 12: 48

Despite her imperfections and shortcomings, I am grateful for the freedoms that have been afforded to me as an American living in America. But as the nation celebrates Independence Day, we must never forget our responsibilities as liberated people.

SAY SOMETHING: FREEDOM IS BIGGER THAN YOU

Psalm 107: 2: *Has the LORD redeemed you? Then speak out! Tell others he has redeemed you from your enemies.* Bob Sorge, in his book *Exploring Worship: A Practical Guide to Praise and Worship,* discusses a concept known as the Horizontal Function of Praise.[17] Essentially, while praise is a vertical interaction between man and God, there are [horizontal] benefits for those in our company. Verses 1 and 2 of the 34th Psalm division (God's Word Translation) illustrate the principle with these words: *I will thank the LORD at all times. My mouth will always praise him. My soul will boast about the LORD. Those who are oppressed will hear it and rejoice.*

Vocal and visible praise are tremendously uplifting to those who are discouraged and despondent. In fact, it was the praise of spiritually free men, Paul and Silas, despite being physically and unfairly shackled, that not only led to their chains being loosed, but also the prisoners around them being set free (Acts 16: 25-26). Friends, like Paul and Silas, are we vehicles for others' freedom? Or, are we guilty of benefiting from the life-changing power of God but hoarding it for ourselves? As we reflect upon our personal freedoms, may we also recognize that there are those who are waiting for us to say something so that they, too, can be free.

BE SOMETHING: FREEDOM HAS PURPOSE

Freedom is more than an opportunity to live comfortably. And while some conveniently view justice as a secondary theme of the Gospel, its entire message is justice. Christ, the central figure of Christianity, was a champion for all people, especially the least of these, by regularly challenging the status quo and upsetting the religious order of the day. It was Christ who was neither afraid nor ashamed to be in the company of those who were considered misfits and excluded from full and meaningful participation with humanity based on artificial rules made by men.

For this reason, we must become champions for those who either do not have a voice of their own, or who are unsure or powerless to effectively speak for themselves. Consider these words that have been attributed to Martin Niemöller, a 20th century pastor and outspoken critic of Adolf Hitler: *First they came for the Socialists, and I did not speak out—Because I was not a Socialist. Then they came for the Trade Unionists, and I did not speak out— Because I was not a Trade Unionist. Then they came for the Jews, and I did not speak out— Because I was not a Jew. Then they came for me—and there was no one left to speak for me.*[18] This eloquent statement is a poignant reminder of what free people must become: change agents. Rather than remaining silent because we are not being discriminated against, or looking to others to fight for justice, free people know that they are the ones who are best positioned to shift cultural paradigms. Even in our own recent history as a nation, the Civil Rights Movement was supported by free people—White people—who were willing to sacrifice the comforts associated with their privileged position for the advancement of marginalized groups.

Friends, are we champions for the least of these? Although we have food to eat, are we the voice for those who are hungry? While we have enough to drink, are we advocates for those who are thirsty? Because we enjoy the company of family and friends, are we extending invitations to those who are alone and lonely? While we have been exonerated, are we forgetting about those who have been wrongfully convicted by an unjust system? Simply stated, freedom is the fulfillment of the timeless words that have been attributed to Mahatma Gandhi: *[we] must be the change [we] wish to see in the world.*[19]

DO SOMETHING: FREEDOM HAS RESPONSIBILITY

When someone has been given much, much will be required in return; and when someone has been entrusted with much, even more will be required (Luke 12: 48). Freedom leads to being an instrument of love and grace. Are we using our un-earned privilege to genuinely and unconditionally love everyone (John 13: 35; 1 John 4: 20-21)? Have our theological perspectives been challenged and better informed so that we truly take on the mind and character of Christ?

If the United States Department of Homeland Security requires individuals to act on behalf of their fellow man by presenting the following challenge—*if you see something, say something*—how much more is expected of us as Christians? Without a doubt, our churches, communities, families, and schools would be forever changed if we, as free people, embodied the words of Dr. Martin Luther King, Jr.: *injustice anywhere is a threat to justice everywhere.*[20]

PERSONAL REFLECTION AND MEDITATION

1. As a free person, what are some ways that you can say something in order to improve the lives of those who have been marginalized by systemic injustice and oppression?

2. As a free person, what are some ways that you can be something in order to improve the lives of those who have been marginalized by systemic injustice and oppression?

3. As a free person, what are some ways that you can do something in order to improve the lives of those who have been marginalized by systemic injustice and oppression?

Thank you for the freedoms that I have been afforded, not only through my relationship with you, but also in the world. Help me to use my privilege to work for justice. Give me the strength to personify the Gospel in everything that I do, especially to challenge systemic oppression and inequity. Amen.

LEST WE FORGET: THE TRAGEDY OF MOVING ON TOO QUICKLY

Then if my people who are called by my name will humble themselves and pray and seek my face and turn from their wicked ways, I will hear from heaven and will forgive their sins and restore their land.

2 Chronicles 7: 14

There is a time for everything, and a season for every activity under the heavens (Ecclesiastes 3:1; New International Version). In light of what transpired throughout 72 painful hours of American history in July 2016, many were asking a multitude of questions. First, why did these tragedies occur? But equally important, what do we do now? Although the second question implies taking the necessary steps to learn and grow from these heinous atrocities that claimed the lives of seven men, it is not meant to minimize the reality that there are hurting children, distraught loved ones, and splintered communities that are still reeling from these terrible events. In no way does it seek to overshadow the excruciating pain of young people who were left without fathers and families suddenly without providers. Yes, we must be careful to not rush the grieving and healing process by moving on too quickly; but we also cannot spend an inordinate amount of time merely glorifying the problem of injustice that continues to plague our nation.

Even as we grapple with this critical challenge, one that is packed with possibility and promise for tomorrow, we should not deceive ourselves that the answer is simple—not that we would want such a response. Instead, we must work to develop and implement a multifaceted strategy that effectively addresses a complex issue such as racism. When the Apostle Paul wrote that we are not wrestling against flesh and blood but against principalities, powers, the rulers of the darkness of this world, and spiritual wickedness in high places (Ephesians 6: 12; King James Version), it is analogous to warring against things that we cannot see—things that transcend what can be discerned with our natural senses. And so it is with racism: a systemic structure of inequity that is maintained by some benefiting while others are necessarily mistreated. For this reason, the problem is not Black people or White people. The problem is not law enforcement or police brutality. The problem will not be addressed through the lens of gun lobbyists, increasing access to mental health treatment, or changing legislation. These things are symptomatic of institutionalized racism, which is embedded within our political, educational, and every other societal system. Although no individual or entity bares the blame for the place in which we find ourselves, it will take everyone's involvement to dismantle a centuries-old establishment.

In responding to a national tragedy in 1994, I heard these words from Rev. DeForest *Buster* Soaries, Jr.: "it boggles my mind and challenges my ministry..." A simple statement, but its profundity continues to echo as I, like many others, seek to not only understand what happened but also what must be done in the days, weeks, and years ahead. As you continue reading, I invite you—Black, White, Native American, Asian, Hispanic, poor, middle class, rich, female, male, gay, straight, transgender—to consider three ways, albeit far from exhaustive, that we can honor the sons, brothers, boyfriends, husbands, and fathers whose lives were lost on July 5, 6, and 7, 2016.

THE ROLE OF THE INDIVIDUAL: IT ALL BEGINS WITH ME

As Jesus shared a meal with his disciples before his impending crucifixion, he told them that one of them would betray him—very soon. Alarmed by this disheartening news, each of them began to ask, *Lord, is it I?* Recorded in Matthew 22: 26, this simple question offers an important lesson: we must always ask ourselves what we did, or did not do, to contribute to our present circumstances. In other words, before expecting anything from anyone, we must consider this fundamental truth: maybe it's me; maybe I'm the problem.

1 Corinthians 13 (vv. 1-8) eloquently speaks about the preeminence of love. And as individuals living in times like these, the best that we can do is demonstrate love. In spite of all that is going on around us, love never fails (v. 8). Very importantly, love has nothing to do with agreeing with others but everything to do with respecting the dignity and humanity of all people. In fact, it was love for all people that ultimately led Christ to voluntarily endure the suffering and

shame of the cross as atonement for all of our shortcomings and sin. Even in these difficult days, do we love as Christ would love—unconditionally regardless of social status, political affiliation, gender identity, sexual orientation, and ethnic group membership?

Additionally, each of us can do something to advance the case for justice. Regardless of being a member of a marginalized group, we can use aspects of our privilege to advocate for someone else. Also in 2016, one of the best examples of this was Officer Nakia Jones' scathing rebuke to her sisters and brothers in blue.[21] Although she is a Black woman and is subjected to discriminatory practices in a variety of ways, Officer Jones used her influential position as a *good cop* to rightfully challenge those who were not upholding their sworn oath to serve and to protect. Brother, sister, you too might be a law enforcement officer. Are you speaking up and speaking out against the criminalization of Black men? And to my White brothers and sisters—those who are not victims of racial profiling and other unfair practices—consider these words from Benjamin Franklin and Martin Luther King, Jr.:

Justice will not be served until those who are unaffected are as outraged as those who are.[22]

I have almost reached the regrettable conclusion that the Negro's great stumbling block in his stride toward freedom is not the Ku Klux Klan but the White moderate who is more devoted to order than to justice.[23]

THE ROLE OF THE COMMUNITY:
THE STRENGTH OF COLLECTIVE UNITY

Through the lens of behavioral psychology, the manner in which Black men are treated in America is a matter of classical and operant conditioning. The majority culture, in many ways, has constantly associated being Black with things that should be feared and that are inherently bad and inferior. While headlines refer to White men who've used guns to assault others as *shooters*, Black men are more often described as *killers*. Albeit subtle, these and other practices have classically conditioned people, even Black people, to fear Black men through their repeated pairings with violence, crime, drugs, aggression, and intimidation. Additionally, the lack of appropriate punishment for those (e.g., some members of law enforcement) who commit crimes against Black men has been reinforcing, which enables these violent acts to continue. Whether intended or not, the absence of an unpleasant consequence communicates that what was done is okay and therefore it happens again, and again, and again.

As community members, we must harness our collective strength by organizing and prioritizing. What is important to us, as Black people in our communities? And, how can we accomplish what we want for our communities? Although voting in federal elections is important, our local officials—county executives, sheriffs, school board members, district attorneys, and county judges—have significantly more influence over our day-to-day lives. The current policies that have led to a disproportionate amount of Black men being killed by police cannot be effectively addressed by the federal government alone. Communities, therefore, must identify injustice and demand change—improved legislation and greater accountability—from their locally elected officials. Sisters and brothers, let's commit to becoming more actively involved in local politics.

Pentecost (Acts 2), an event that forever changed the course of history through the birth of the New Testament Church, was the result of a group of people who were gathered in one place and who shared the same vision. The place in which we find ourselves calls for unity—not Black unity, but human unity. Let's organize our communities and ourselves so that we can experience the collective strength and impact that is only possible by having a singular purpose and goal.

THE ROLE OF THE CHURCH: THE CENTRALITY OF THE GOSPEL

A passive approach to Christianity is an indictment on the living and breathing Body of Christ. Passive Christianity—a belief that God will take care of everything while we pray and have faith in his power to do the impossible—is a convenient and lazy excuse to not do and become all that he requires of us (Matthew 5: 13-16). For example, the 14th verse of 2 Chronicles 7 is often referenced in the aftermath of national tragedies. And while it admonishes us to humble ourselves, pray, and seek the face of God, it also says that we must turn from our wicked ways. In other words, coupled with praying—for justice and for God to change the hearts of people throughout the land—he also expects us to do things differently (James 2: 14-26).

It would be tremendously insensitive to move on too quickly—of resuming business as usual in our quest to restore normalcy. While many houses of worship likely referenced the awful events during their initial weekend services, what about now? Because news stories and social media activity are focused on other things, has The Church, which has been charged with advocating for justice and the least of these, followed suit? In the same manner that Advent is a season and is celebrated over 4 weeks, we, as a people and a nation, are in a season that cannot be limited to a single week's cursory acknowledgment. What, then, should churches do?

For those of us who boast of our sensitivity to the leading of the Holy Spirit, pastors and church leaders should consider suspending their sermon series, especially if they are not salient to the realities of the current socio-cultural climate. Because the Holy Spirit is alive and responsive to what we need, at times he will interrupt our best laid plans. Let's pray that our church leaders would be both sensitive and courageous enough to hear and follow the leading of the Holy Spirit so that we won't miss what needs to be said in this pivotal and prophetic moment. Relatedly, as a former music director, parishioners occasionally asked me about the process of identifying worship service selections. My response was that the songs sung had very little to do with what I liked or what was in heavy rotation on the radio. Instead, I would ask the Lord what he wanted to hear. The One who is touched by our feelings, our emotions, our hurt, and our pain would want to hear songs that encourage those who are afraid and filled with questions. Although the Gospel is not a fairy tale, it is Good News. For this reason, more than ever before, The Church must be intentional about giving their congregants the hope that is found in Jesus Christ. Regardless of all that is happening around us, *The Lord of Hosts is with us and the God of Jacob is our refuge* (Psalm 46; King James Version). And even though *we are pressed on every side by troubles, we are not crushed. We are perplexed, but not driven to despair. We are hunted down, but never abandoned by God. We get knocked down, but we are not destroyed* (2 Corinthians 4: 8 & 9).

As a Black man living in 21st century America, I never imagined that I would be experiencing, firsthand, what is going around me. These problems should have been solved by now. These things, reminiscent of the tumultuous and turbulent 1960's, should not be happening. But alas, they are and we must find the strength to work towards better. Although difficult, this requires the work of challenging ourselves, first as individuals; working together, with all people, as communities; and the Body of Christ proclaiming the Good News of the Gospel in both word and deed. Paraphrased from Galatians 6: 9, let's not get tired of doing what is right; because eventually we will see the results and it will be worth it. Regardless of how uncomfortable, let's not abandon this place—this difficult place of suffering. Let's not abandon this place of pain. But let's work through it, together. Let's learn from it, together. Let's grow from it, together.

Walk together children, and don't get weary.

PERSONAL REFLECTION AND MEDITATION

1. In working for justice, what is your role as an individual? What can you do to challenge institutionalized oppression (e.g., classism, homophobia, racism, sexism, and xenophobia) and advance the cause of justice in your respective spheres of influence?

2. In working for justice, what is your role as a community member? How can you partner with others in your community to hold your elected officials accountable for the policies and practices that affect you and your neighbors?

3. In working for justice, what is your role as a member of a faith community? How can your organize with other Christians to tangibly demonstrate the love of Christ to everyone?

Thank you for giving me the desire to serve others. Help me to never be satisfied with only praying about injustice. Give me the strength to work for justice. Amen.

CAN I TRUST YOU?

*More than being gifted young people, David and Joseph understood
that their supernatural abilities were not for their own benefit,
but rather should be used to help others.*

It's always exciting to hear children talking about what they want to be when
they grow up. While some aspire to become firemen or police officers, others
hope to be doctors, lawyers, or world famous athletes. When asked why they
have these goals for their lives, children's responses are likely based on superfici-
alities such as having fun, making a lot of money, or being adored by millions
of fans. Although these reasons are developmentally appropriate, and perhaps
even expected, as we mature into adulthood, we must put away our egocentric
ways of thinking and relating to the world around us (1 Corinthians 13: 11).

CAN I TRUST YOU WITH THIS GIFT?

Everyone has a gift—the supernatural ability to do something well without
significant stress or undue effort. For some it may be painting. For others it
could be excelling in various academic subjects or sporting events. As adults,
one of our greatest responsibilities is to help young people identify and fully
develop their God-given talents. Importantly, after children recognize the areas
in which they have been gifted, they can take advantage of opportunities that
are aligned with these abilities rather than pursuing paths that are incompatible
with how they have been uniquely created. In other words, the nexus of a person's gift with a chance to use it is not only the place of divine purpose, but also
true happiness and fulfillment beyond the temporary trappings of success. Let's
consider two important questions. First, what gift has God given me? Next,
what does he want me to do with it?

GIFTED FOR A PURPOSE: LESSONS FROM DAVID AND JOSEPH

In Proverbs 18: 16 we read that a man's gift makes room for him and brings him before great men. Said another way, the gift that God has given you, and me, will open doors of tremendous opportunity. When David was asked to play his harp, which soothed Saul's tormented spirit (1 Samuel 16: 14-23), the young shepherd-boy musician went from the obscurity of tending his father's sheep to the king's palace—not because he presented himself, but rather his gift made room for him.

Having been favored by his father and because he was a dreamer, Joseph was hated by his brothers who also plotted to kill him (Genesis 37: 3-4; 18-21). After being sold into Egyptian slavery (vv. 27-28), Joseph found himself in Potiphar's house (Genesis 39: 1-2). Although Potiphar liked Joseph and placed him in charge of his affairs (vv. 4-6), Potiphar's wife tried to seduce him (vv. 7-9). Despite Joseph maintaining his integrity and refusing her advances, she lied about him to her husband, which led to his unjust imprisonment (vv. 10-20). But while he was in prison, Joseph interpreted a series of dreams that no one—not even the wise men and magicians—could discern (Genesis 40: 12-13; Genesis 41: 8; 39-44). As a result, he was placed in a position of prominence; and when a great famine occurred, the Egyptians had enough to eat (vv. 54-56).

More than being gifted young people, David and Joseph understood that their supernatural abilities were not for their own benefit, but rather should be used to help others. David, through his musical giftedness, effectively ministered to Saul. And because Joseph continued to use his gift of interpreting dreams despite being unfairly jailed, he was instrumental in Egypt's sustenance while other nations were starving. David and Joseph show that regardless of our present circumstances, and when others may not recognize our gifts, in the fullness of time, God will orchestrate divine opportunities so that we can use what he gave us, not for our own benefit, but to encourage others.

TO WHOM MUCH IS GIVEN, EVEN MORE IS REQUIRED

In 2016, as summer was winding down and the National Football League (NFL) was opening its season, our Facebook, Twitter, and Instagram feeds may have been filled with images of Colin Kaepernick, the San Francisco 49ers quarterback who refused to stand during the national anthem. But in addition to taking a knee during this song, Mr. Kaepernick pledged $1M of his earnings to support community organizations and contributed towards $60K worth of backpacks for children returning to school in New York City. Despite anyone's opinion of Mr. Kaepernick's decision to exercise his first amendment rights, the significance of a mainstream celebrity raising awareness about race-based injustice and inequity is critically important. Like David and Joseph, because he was given something special—the ability and opportunity to become a professional athlete—he also had a moral imperative to use his name, money, fame, and influence for the betterment of all people.

THE CHANCE OF A LIFETIME

Because we are no longer children, now what? To borrow a metaphor from politics, what is our platform? Having been afforded positions of prominence, what do we want to accomplish for others by using the gifts that God has given us?

Jesus says these words in Matthew 5: 13-16: *You are the salt of the earth. But what good is salt if it has lost its flavor? …You are the light of the world—like a city on a hilltop that cannot be hidden. No one lights a lamp and then puts it under a basket. Instead, a lamp is placed on a stand, where it gives light to everyone in the house. In the same way, let your good deeds shine out for all to see, so that everyone will praise your heavenly Father.* As Christ challenged the religious and social order of the day, especially by being a champion for the least of these (Matthew 25: 40), we must also be change agents. Our homes, families, communities, houses of worship, workplaces, and schools should be better because of our presence. Like David and Joseph were inextricably connected to improving the quality of life for those in their respective spheres of influence, it's our time to use what God has given us to do the same.

Because it only takes one person to start a movement, can I trust you?

PERSONAL REFLECTION AND MEDITATION

1. Use this space to write your thoughts and reflections on this essay.

2. What was especially meaningful to you?

3. Identify at least one gift that God has you. How are you using your gift to serve others?

Thank for you for enabling me to do something

exceptionally well. Help me to never take my

gifts for granted, but to always use them to help

others. Thank you for giving me opportunities

to use my gifts to improve the lives of those who

are less fortunate. Amen.

FOR
STUDENTS AND
EDUCATORS

BEHIND THE SCENES

As school systems are working behind the scenes for their students,
God is also working behind the scenes for us.

Children almost always eagerly anticipate the closing of the school year. For some, school days in May and June are merely inconvenient annoyances to blissful summer days and endless summer nights. But while vacations are necessary for rest, relaxation, and rejuvenation, a lot happens during the break from books, bells, assignments, and assessments.

In working for a public school system, I've learned that there is constant preparation from the moment one school year ends and another begins. Physically, classrooms are cleaned as old, dilapidated furniture is removed, only to be replaced with new desks, new chairs, and shampooed rugs. Walls receive fresh coats of paint and floors are waxed to perfection. While some staff members are informed that they will no longer enjoy the privilege of employment, others are reassigned to make better use of their skills. For teachers and administrators, there are numerous professional development opportunities to learn effective strategies and other cutting edge advancements to serve their students. These things, however, are happening unbeknownst to the boys and girls who will benefit from such careful planning and intentional preparation. When students enter spotless buildings and experience curriculum adjustments, new initiatives, programs, and even people who will patiently work with them, they have no idea that an entire system, like a well-oiled machine, has been working behind the scenes for their good.

As school systems are working behind the scenes for their students, God is also working behind the scenes for us. Although we may not see it, he is shifting people and situations—all for our good (Romans 8: 28). Because we live by faith rather than what we can discern with our natural senses (2 Corinthians 5: 7), even when it feels like God is not there, always remember that he's an ever-present help in trouble (Psalm 46: 1)—one who works behind the scenes for you and me.

PERSONAL REFLECTION AND MEDITATION

1. Use this space to write your thoughts and reflections on this essay.

2. What was especially meaningful to you?

Thank you for always working on my behalf. Even when I don't recognize that you are moving heaven and earth for me, increase my faith to place my confidence in you. Amen.

ALTERING PUBLIC SPACE

Around midnight Paul and Silas were praying and singing hymns to God,
and the other prisoners were listening. Suddenly, there was a massive earthquake,
and the prison was shaken to its foundations. All the doors immediately
flew open, and the chains of every prisoner fell off!

Acts 16: 25-26

Brent Staples' "Just Walk On By: A Black Man Ponders His Power To Alter Public Space" is a relatively short, yet poignant piece about the realities facing Black men in America.[24] First published in a 1986 issue of *Ms. Magazine,* Staples eloquently articulates his ability to alter public space. As he recounts personal experiences of hearing the "thunk" of drivers locking their car doors upon his arrival in a crosswalk; being mistaken for a burglar in an office building; and seeing women with "their purse straps strung across their chests bandolier style... bracing themselves against being tackled," however unfortunate, these were lived experiences for Staples, a college-educated, Black man in America. Perhaps even more disappointing, these scenarios and more continue to be true for Black men living in America. No doubt a sad commentary, Black men, forever aware of their perceived intimidating presence, are forced to accept their uncanny ability to alter the environments that they enter. As a Black man living in America, it is virtually impossible to not, at least once, think about my Blackness—my identity, the essence of who I am—as a burden. But as a Christian, a committed follower of Christ, I must also consider whether my presence has the same power to alter the environments in which I live, work, and play.

The Book of Acts chronicles the birth of the New Testament Church. In chapter 1 (v. 8), Christ instructs his disciples to preach the Gospel throughout the world. In chapter 2, the Holy Spirit indwells, endows, and empowers 120 individuals with the supernatural ability to speak in such a way that people from various ethnicities were able to hear and respond to the Gospel message (vv. 1-6). Later in the same chapter (vv. 14-41), we read about Peter's sermon that led to the salvation of 3,000 new Christians. These demonstrations made the apostles—those who literally walked and talked with Christ—quite credible in the community. In verses 12 through 16 of chapter 5 we read about the miracles that were performed by these men through the power and presence of the Holy Spirit operating in their lives. Verse 15 (New International Version), however, is particularly meaningful: *As a result, people brought the sick into the streets and laid them on beds and mats so that at least Peter's shadow might fall on some of them as he passed by.*

Like Staples' Blackness, the presence of Peter's shadow had the ability to affect change. Not because of his own greatness, but the power of God operating in his life, those who were sick and in need of divine intervention simply wanted to be close enough to Peter so that they could experience healing virtue through his shadow. Friends, does our presence alter public space? Are the places that we visit better because we've been there? Are we changing the public spaces of our families and the dynamics of our communities? Does our presence change the atmosphere and lives of those around us?

Without a doubt, Christ remains the most significant change agent in history. Not only is time (BC and AD) anchored by his existence, but his name, Jesus, is also centered on redeeming humankind from everlasting damnation (Matthew 1: 21). By atoning for our sins, his death affords us access to a changed and eternal life (John 3: 16). And as his disciples who have been charged to take on his character, we must also do what he did (John 14: 12). Friends, how are we changing the public spaces that we occupy?

Some time ago, I came across a tremendously inspiring article on my Facebook newsfeed. Posted by MRSACKLEY, and especially relevant for my colleagues who are teachers, administrators, and most of all school psychologists (smile) during this exciting time of back-to-school, "When God Is in The Classroom" was an encouraging reminder that the manner in which we serve our students is a reflection of our relationship with God.[25] Because children were special to Christ (Matthew 19: 14), when we advocate for the provision of their most basic needs, protect them from the evils of injustice, patiently teach them the skills they need to be successful, and instill in them the importance of serving others, we are demonstrating the love of God.

As the presence of Paul and Silas in a Philippian jail (Acts 16) altered the public space around them, may the presence of the Lord not only change us, but the places we go and those whom we encounter.

PERSONAL REFLECTION AND MEDITATION

1. Think about the places that you live, work, and play. What healthy qualities are missing from these environments? For example, are they lacking love? Are they lacking peace?

2. How can your presence in these settings alter these public spaces?

3. Identify one way that you can consistently demonstrate the character of Christ to influence your home or work environment.

———◗•●•◖———

Thank you for always being with me. Thank you that my presence can change atmospheres and influence those around me. Help me to never forget the power that rests in me to be an agent of love, peace, and grace. Amen.

———◗•●•◖———

DROWNING IN SHALLOW WATER

The temptations in your life are no different from what others experience. And God is faithful. He will not allow the temptation to be more than you can stand. When you are tempted, he will show you a way out so that you can endure.

1 Corinthians 10: 13

Written by Theodor Seuss Geisel, better known as Dr. Seuss, and published by Random House in 1954, *Horton Hears A Who* begins with these words: "On the 15th of May, in the Jungle of Nool, in the heat of the day, in the cool of the pool, he was splashing... enjoying the jungle's great joys... when Horton the elephant heard a small noise."[26] For me, it was the evening of July 23rd and I was in a hotel pool, not splashing, but nonetheless enjoying a mini-vacation with my family when the Lord spoke to me about drowning in shallow water. Because it was no more than four feet deep, the message resonated with me even more. Further, as drowning can happen as a result of very little water entering a person's lungs, children have drowned in bathtubs, and adults under the influence of drugs and alcohol have succumbed to drowning in puddles.

In Judges 13, we are introduced to more than a fictitious Biblical figure with presumably long, flowing locks of hair. Samson, although his strength was somewhat mythical, was a real man, living in a real world, facing real challenges. Like David, the anointed musician and faithful shepherd who despite wrestling a lion, a bear, and defeating a giant (1 Samuel 17: 34-37; 49-50) could not resist a married woman (2 Samuel 11: 2-4), Samson, despite killing a thousand men with the jawbone of a donkey (Judges 15: 15-16), went to see a harlot (Judges 16: 1). Like some of us today, Samson and David were drowning in shallow water. As voyeurs into the life of Samson, Judges 16 (vv. 6-20) highlights aspects of his personality that led to an unfortunate outcome.

LIVING ON THE EDGE

Samson might be described as an edge dweller—one who enjoyed the thrill of flirting with risky situations. Because of this, he played a dangerous game of cat-and-mouse with Delilah. But as he placed himself in perilous predicaments, he did not recognize that he was on the verge of losing everything. And rather than guarding the gift that God gave him, Samson carelessly exploited it and lost. In other words, Samson played with fire and got burned. In Judges 16 we read that Samson toyed with Delilah about the secret to his strength, not once or twice, but four times (vv. 7, 11, 13, 17).

BEING OVERCONFIDENT

In addition to being an edge dweller, Samson was overconfident. Because of his supernatural strength, did he think that he was too strong to fail? Even today, how many of us drown in shallow water because we underestimate the strength and weight of sin?

While standing in an area of the beach that was barely waist deep, I was overpowered, multiple times, by what my wife called an angry sea. Despite my intentions to simply enjoy the beauty and warmth of the water, my human strength was no match for the waves controlled by the All-Powerful Architect of Creation. And so it is with sin: that which is enticing to the eyes, in a moment, can literally knock us off of our feet, bring us to our knees, and carry us farther than we ever intended until we are drifting in an everlasting abyss. As Bishop Norman Lyons has appropriately said about sin, "You either deal with it, or it will deal with you."

ABUSING GRACE

In the words of Pastor Curtis Thompson, Samson was also an abuser of grace. Said another way, he took advantage of the grace that was extended to him, which also inadvertently reinforced his risky behavior. Yes, grace ensures that we don't experience what we deserve (punishment) but rather what we need (love and forgiveness). But some of us misinterpret the absence of punishment for sin as God's approval of what we are doing. We even rationalize, *if God didn't punish me, then it must not be sin.* Nothing, however, could be further from the truth, even as Paul cautions us against such errant thinking in Romans 6: 1-2. Like Samson, most people don't intend to drown—especially in puddles or bathtubs. But the repeated playing with grace, coupled with living on the edge, and being overly confident in our own strength while underestimating the weight and persuasive power of sin, will most assuredly lead to our demise. Friends: drowning in shallow water is not the byproduct of colossal circumstances but the seemingly insignificant episodes that ultimately consume us, although they shouldn't.

YOU DON'T HAVE TO DROWN

Because the beginning of school is one of the most exciting times of the year, I would like to encourage young people with these words: don't drown in shallow water! As a school psychologist, I've sat in too many meetings, with too many students who have allowed themselves to be overtaken by things that were well within their control. Having met with them to discuss how their parents and teachers can best support their success, and having access to numerous interventions and accommodations, some refuse the assistance. In fact, when asked if their assignments were too difficult, many said that they simply chose not to do their work. As a result, they drown in shallow water. Although it could have been avoided, they fail and jeopardize their future.

Young people, this year can be different. Don't allow anything or anyone, especially your own choices, to cause you to drown in shallow water. Many of you have worked too hard to get to your final year in high school or college. And even if you're not a senior, you have sacrificed too much to drown in shallow water. As Samson eventually ran out of time and could not withstand his attackers (Judges 16: 20-21), don't let it be too late for you. Rather than procrastinating, do all that you can to get ahead and remain ahead throughout the school year.

As drowning begins with only a little bit of water, remember that problems arise when we slowly dig a hole for ourselves that eventually becomes too deep to escape.

PERSONAL REFLECTION AND MEDITATION

1. Ask the Lord to show you if you are an edge dweller, being overconfident, or abusing of grace. If so, ask him to forgive you and show you how to live differently. What specific steps can you take to make better decisions?

2. If you are an edge dweller, being overconfident, or abusing grace, prayerfully consider someone to whom you can be accountable for your actions.

---◀)•●•(▶---

Thank you for loving me enough to show me my shortcomings. Help me to live in a manner that honors you. Help me to make decisions that are healthy, not only individually, but also for my family. Amen.

---◀)•●•(▶---

ON BEING A MISFIT

We were not designed to fit and it's okay to be a misfit.

As a second grader, Alex was reading on grade level. But as he got older, his skills did not improve. Because Alex was maintaining, some felt that his reading was not getting worse. This, however, was not only inaccurate, but also impossible. In virtually every area of our lives, getting older bears the expectation of improving. Therefore, maintaining is synonymous with regression. In other words, if we're not getting better, we're getting worse. Likewise, if we're simply maintaining our relationship with God, rather than becoming more like him, this is also concerning.

While growth is both healthy and necessary, it is also uncomfortable. As students are returning to school, some may feel nervous about meeting new teachers and peers. Others may become anxious about the increased academic and social demands of a new grade. *Will I understand the work? Will I be able to complete my assignments on time? How much homework will they give me? Will I be able to find my classes? Will I make new friends?* These questions are related to being a misfit. And although the term connotes being excluded from certain groups, let's consider three reasons why we were not designed to fit and why it's okay to be a misfit.

WE ARE TOO BIG FOR WHERE WE WERE

The initial days of a new school year may be somewhat intimidating, especially for students who are transitioning to new buildings. Those leaving elementary school for middle school, or middle school for high school, have traded their familiar surroundings and status of being big fish in little ponds for what feels like goldfish in a sea of the unknown.

Educators often use terms such as mastery, frustration, and instructional to describe the degree of difficulty their students are experiencing with academic tasks. Whereas mastery is indicative of assignments being too easy, frustration communicates that concepts are too difficult. The sweet spot, however, is the instructional level: the place at which the student is appropriately challenged without becoming discouraged because things are too complicated, or bored because they're too simple.

For students entering new grades or new schools, this is scary—at least for the moment. But over time, as they learn the rules and routines of their new settings, they realize that where they are now, is actually where they should be. Yes, sixth grade might be somewhat daunting; but fifth grade was too easy for me. Yes, the social scene in college is going to take some getting used to; but I've grown beyond what high school had to offer.

As people who are constantly evolving throughout our spiritual development, we often feel like misfits. Nevertheless, be encouraged. We were not designed to fit and it's okay to be a misfit. In fact, discomfort is a necessary prelude to growth. The uneasiness that we feel when the Lord places us in unfamiliar situations is his way of ensuring that we are never, ever, only maintaining, but always growing.

WE ARE TOO SMALL FOR WHERE WE ARE

Coupled with being too big for where we once were, we are also too small for where we are now. Said another way, although students have met the requirements to pass eighth grade, this does not always mean that they are fully comfortable being high school freshmen.

In some systems, youngsters are assessed at the beginning of the year to determine their baseline knowledge before they're exposed to the curriculum. And periodically, evaluations are used to monitor their progress toward end of year objectives. By comparing their performance in the fall to their achievement in the spring, if there has been a positive change, instruction has been effective and students have learned—they've grown!

Friends, it's okay to be a misfit because we are never expected to have all of the answers. Yes, we are too big for where we were; but we are still growing into all that we will eventually become. Don't worry. In time, the Lord will show us, teach us, and expose us to everything we need in order to become more like him.

WE ARE EXACTLY WHERE WE NEED TO BE

Despite being frustrated and overwhelmed by the uncertainty that surrounds us, be encouraged: where we are, is exactly where we need to be. In fact, this is our instructional level: the place at which we will continue learning and growing into what God desires us to be. Because he never gives us more than we can handle (1 Corinthians 10: 13), let's trust the manner in which the Lord develops our Christian character so that we are more loving, more patient, showing more kindness, and demonstrating greater self-control (Galatians 5: 22-23).

Because life is about change, and change takes time, let's not rush to become more than who we are right now. Consider this: although David was anointed to be king (1 Samuel 16: 7-13), he spent years as a misfit before he assumed this position at 30 years old (2 Samuel 5: 4). Similar to our own lived experiences, while David was in obscurity—tending his father's sheep; playing his harp to soothe Saul's tormented spirit (1 Samuel 16: 21-23); serving his brothers, which led to defeating Goliath (1 Samuel 17: 17-18; 26-51); developing a close friendship with Jonathan who protected him on several occasions (1 Samuel 18: 1-4; 1 Samuel 20: 9-13); and respecting a jealous and insecure leader who was trying to kill him (1 Samuel 18: 1-12; 19: 10)—the Lord was developing and refining his Christian character. Despite being a misfit, through every situation, every challenge, and every fearful moment, David was growing out of where he was and into where God wanted him to be.

Trust the process.

PERSONAL REFLECTION AND MEDITATION

1. Use this space to write your thoughts and reflections on this essay.

2. What was especially meaningful to you?

3. For which places or situations are you too big?

4. For which places and situations are you too small?

Thank you for always being with me. Thank you for using all of my experiences to refine my character and make me into the person that you want me to be. Help me to not rush the process, but to trust the process. Amen.

THANKSGIVING

A THANKSGIVING MEDITATION

I can't do more for you until I know that you appreciate what I've already done.

It is a disheartening reality that each year the commercialization of Christmas creeps upon us sooner and sooner. It's as if we make a quantum leap from the end of summer celebrations on Labor Day to the shopping frenzies of Black Friday having made our lists and checked them twice. It is an indictment on our culture that hardly takes a moment to thank God for his many blessings. While Thanksgiving Day is given a cursory glance, Christmas receives a stare.

The 14th chapter of Matthew (vv. 17-20) chronicles Jesus' miraculous feeding of more than 5,000 people. The Amplified Bible says it this way:

They (the disciples) said to Him (Jesus), "We have nothing here but five loaves and two fish." He said, "Bring them here to Me." Then He ordered the crowds to recline on the grass; and He took the five loaves and the two fish, and, looking up to heaven, He gave thanks and blessed and broke the loaves and handed the pieces to the disciples, and the disciples gave them to the people. And they all ate and were satisfied. And they picked up twelve baskets full of the broken pieces left over.

I am convinced that the ability to feed a multitude of 5,000 men, women, and children with a little boy's lunch was first and foremost predicated upon saying *Thank You*. In this season, let us take a moment to think about two simple words that have immeasurable impact when used together.

THANK YOU KEEPS THINGS IN PROPER PERSPECTIVE

Not only is this phrase symbolic of appreciation and gratitude, it also express the sentiment found in Galatians 2: 20 (King James Version): *Not I, but Christ.* In other words, it speaks of total dependence on God. For example, when, by the grace of God, we have been used to advance The Kingdom, thank you keeps the focus where it ultimately belongs. Rather than deceiving ourselves into thinking that it was by our own strength and capabilities, thank you reminds us that we can do nothing without God operating in our lives. Further, thank you is the embodiment of, *Lord, you didn't have to do this but I'm glad you did.* Although we might not have the jobs that we would like or the homes in which we want to raise our families, nevertheless, we say, *Thank You, Jesus! In spite of my shortcomings, you have been good to me!* As Christ gave thanks for what he already had, he was also positioning himself to receive what God would do through him.

THANK YOU LEAVES ROOM FOR MORE

Thank you is the key that unlocks the door to what is seemingly impossible and prepares the way for supernatural miracles. Consider this: When did Christ give thanks? It was first. In fact, the text doesn't indicate that he asked for more food. The simple act of being thankful led to receiving more than enough to meet the need of the crowd. Even today, rather than asking God to do more for us, consider this message: *I can't do more for you until I know that you appreciate what I've already done.* As parents bare the responsibility of teaching their children the importance of showing good manners, especially saying please and thank you, youngsters have often experienced a favorable response after using these simple and kind words. It's as if those who hear them say thank you think, "How can I not give her more [food] or another [toy]? She appreciates what I've already done so she must be ready for more!" And so it is with God. Instead of waiting for him to display his supernatural power, we should be thanking God for what we already have. Thanking God for what he has already done in our lives shows that we are faithful stewards over what we presently have and are ready to appropriately handle additional blessings.

HE WANTS TO HEAR IT FROM YOU

Matthew, Mark, and Luke each record the account of the nine lepers who failed to say thank you after Jesus had healed them. Although a common interpretation of these passages is that they were ungrateful by not acknowledging the source of their deliverance, there are other lessons to be learned from this parable. Because they were lepers and consequently marginalized from others in society, now that they were healed, those whom they encountered likely knew that something supernatural had taken place. Therefore, it is plausible that they told others about their life-changing experience with Jesus. Telling others, however, was not enough.

As the Lord delights in the praises of his people (Psalm 22:3), in its simplest form, praise is saying thank you. And because he wants to hear it from you, this year, above everything else and before everything else, tell God thank you.

PERSONAL REFLECTION AND MEDITATION

1. Identify 3-5 things for which you are thankful.

2. Make a conscious decision to specifically thank God for these things.

3. Rather than asking God for anything, spend the next few moments thanking God for what you identified above (see #1), as well as anything else that comes to your mind.

Thank you for everything. Amen.

IT TOOK ALL OF THAT
TO GET TO THIS

Dear brothers and sisters, when troubles come your way, consider it an opportunity for great joy. For you know that when your faith is tested, your endurance has a chance to grow. So let it grow, for when your endurance is fully developed, you will be perfect and complete, needing nothing.

James 1: 1-4

Although each of us can likely think of several reasons for why we are thankful, disappointing news about our health and less than ideal financial situations are typically not in the forefront of our minds. But whether we are expecting God to do great things, or we find ourselves enjoying what he has already done, consider these words: it took all of that to get to this. During this season of thanksgiving, let's consider three reasons for being thankful.

I AM THANKFUL FOR GRACE AND MERCY

As people, it is comforting to say that *A causes B*. While students want to know that their hours spent studying will indefinitely lead to a stellar grade on their next exam, school psychologists seek to make causal linkages between their creatively crafted interventions and subsequent successful outcomes. But despite how appealing these direct connections might be, they are far less frequent than we are willing to admit. In other words, life is filled with complex, sometimes messy, interactions rather than direct relationships.

Even related to spiritual matters, human nature predisposes us to think in overly simplistic terms of cause and effect. For example, if the Lord blessed me, it must have been the result of what I did. And if something unfortunate happened to me, similarly, I must have done something to upset God. Not only is such thinking unhealthy and contrary to the nature of an ever-loving God, nothing could be further from the truth. As it is in life, much of the Christian experience cannot be traced to, or predicted by, what we have or have not done. Because of grace, which is beyond our control, we have access to things that we don't deserve. In the same manner, because of mercy, we don't always bear the negative consequences of our actions (Lamentations 3: 22). To borrow a term from research methodology, grace and mercy are confounding variables that muddy the direct path between what we do and what we receive in return. Psalm 103: 10-12:

> *He does not punish us for all our sins; he does not deal harshly with us, as we deserve. For his unfailing love toward those who fear him is as great as the height of the heavens above the earth. He has removed our sins as far from us as the east is from the west.*

I AM THANKFUL BECAUSE IT WAS GOOD FOR ME

While it is safe to assume that no one wants to be stressed, such thinking has influenced our expectation of the Christian life: it should only be filled with perpetual comfort and happiness. Pain and suffering, however, are not only inevitable, but they are also necessary. As one who did not always appreciate the value of my challenges while in the midst of them, I eventually learned, like the psalmist, that these things were good for me (Psalm 119: 71). In many ways, life, especially the Christian life, is about growing—being better today than we were yesterday. And although we can learn from the mistakes of others, sometimes experience is the best teacher.

Difficult days and tough times serve a two-fold purpose: they teach us about God and they teach us about ourselves. Because God desires intimate fellowship with each of us, he is committed to doing whatever is necessary in pursuit of such a relationship, including allowing us to endure hardship. In fact, many of us can attest to our most consistent conversations with God occurring in the midst of adversity. So if it took all of that to strengthen our relationship with God, not only was it good for us, it was worth it!

Difficulty perfects our Christian character. Although we assume the likeness of Christ—love, joy, peace, patience, kindness, goodness, faithfulness, gentleness, and self-control (Galatians 5: 22-23)—as a function of our relationship with him, these qualities do not develop automatically. Instead, the Lord uses situations that we encounter in our day-to-day lives to mature these attributes that are central to our Christian character. In other words, when love is lacking, he places us in uncomfortable situations in which we must become more loving. If we are lacking patience, he gives us opportunities to exercise and strengthen our existing, albeit weaker, patience. To grow in kindness, gentleness, and self-control, God intentionally inconveniences us so that we can demonstrate these qualities to our friends, families, and even our so-called enemies.

I AM THANKFUL BECAUSE ALL THINGS ARE WORKING TOGETHER

Although the Bible is far from a fairy tale, our *once upon a time* beginnings ultimately lead to *happily ever after* endings. Joseph, for example, once upon a time was rejected by his brothers, thrown into a pit, lied on by Potiphar's wife, and imprisoned for unjust, unfair, and indefensible reasons (Genesis 37, 39, & 40). But if it weren't for these seemingly unfortunate events, he would have never reached the place that God had predestined for him (Genesis 41). Like you and I today, it took all of that for Joseph to arrive at his prepared place of promise.

Some time ago, Pastor Anthony Ferguson posted the following on his Facebook page: *God does not waste pain. He uses it to accomplish his purpose.* These simple sentences contain the realization that nothing is casual or by happenstance. Personally speaking, in 2006 I relocated to Northern Virginia, a place in which I never thought that I would be living. And although I am no longer doing what led me to the area, it took all of that to get to my current situation. As much as I would like to draw causal connections between my decisions and the place in which I find myself—ministering wholeness to those whom I have the privilege of serving each day—it was a series of divinely orchestrated steps (Psalm 37: 2) that brought me through all of that to get to this. Even the steps that were taken through the valley of the shadow of death (Psalm 23: 4); these were not designed to kill me but to make me better. So rather than becoming discouraged, despondent, upset, and unsettled by everything that we go through, we should celebrate because God does not waste anything. He takes our pain and transforms it into power. He takes our hurt and allows it to be instrumental in others' healing.

More than what you are thankful for, why are you thankful? Today, I'm thankful for the grace and mercy of God that confounds everything about my life and overwhelms me over, and over, and over again. I'm thankful that everything I've experienced was good for me. But most of all, although I don't always understand what he's doing, I'm thankful that God does all things well.

Because it took all of that to get to this, trust the process.

PERSONAL REFLECTION AND MEDITATION

1. Think about at least one situation in which you were frustrated while going through a challenging circumstance. Having made it to the other side, what are you thankful for that perhaps you didn't appreciate in the moment?

2. Even when you are going through challenging situations, how can you remain thankful?

Thank you for ordering my steps. Help me to know that you are leading me to a prepared place, despite what I feel about my current circumstances. Amen.

GRATEFUL FOR GRACE

God saved you by his grace when you believed.
And you can't take credit for this; it is a gift from God.

Ephesians 2: 8

Thanksgiving is a moment to pause and reflect. Having made it through 11 months of another year, we've certainly experienced good days and bad days; happy times and sad times; setbacks and successes. Nevertheless, we're still standing. And because we're still standing, we have something for which we can be thankful. But as we're recalling and recounting our blessings, we should also be grateful for what makes these things possible: grace. In looking closer, let's consider 5 qualities of grace.

GIVES

Fundamentally, we cannot earn God's grace; it is a gift that is freely given to us. Ephesians 2: 8-9 and John 3:16:

> *God saved you by his grace when you believed. And you can't take credit for this; it is a gift from God. Salvation is not a reward for the good things we have done, so none of us can boast about it.*

> *For this is how God loved the world: He gave his one and only Son, so that everyone who believes in him will not perish but have eternal life.*

Taken together, these scriptures not only show that grace gives, but it gives generously.

Further, grace gives voluntarily. Especially for those who cannot or will not ask for themselves (Matthew 25: 35-40), grace gives food to the hungry. Grace willingly gives water to our sisters and brothers who are thirsty and clothes to those who are naked. Without a personal invitation, grace takes care of our neighbors who are sick and visits those who are imprisoned so that they are never alone or forgotten. And for those who do not look like us, but are living in unsafe and life-threatening conditions, grace welcomes them by providing a place of refuge and safety.

Today, how can we generously and voluntarily give to others?

RESTORES

Recorded in Luke 15 (vv. 11-32), the *Parable of The Lost Son* is not only a narrative of redemption, but more importantly restoration. After demanding and squandering his inheritance by living irresponsibly and recklessly (vv. 12-13), grace accounts for what happens upon the prodigal son's return to his father's house. Seeing that his son was on his way home, the father ran to meet him, kissed him, and embraced him (v. 20). And when he was home, the father gave his son the finest robe, a ring, and sandals (v. 22). In other words, because grace restores, the son didn't have to start over but was allowed to continue the life that he knew before he left home. Because grace gives generously and voluntarily, without having to earn his father's favor or asking for anything, the son received all of the emblems that were indicative of his enduring sonship.

Although the father was likely hurt and disappointed by his son's poor choices, he did not allow these things to stand in the way of their relationship. Friends, isn't this what God does for us? Despite our disobedience, he is committed to restoring us by his faithful and unconditional love.

Today, some of us have relationships that need to be reconciled. Instead of holding grudges, how can we actively restore others by offering them the same grace that we have been given?

ACCEPTS

While an anonymous woman was getting water from a well, the manner in which Christ spoke to her showed that grace accepts everyone (John 4: 1-42). In other words, grace sees what we shall be rather than who we are in our current stage of spiritual maturity. Notably, Jesus, who was Jewish, wasn't supposed to interact with the woman because she was a Samaritan (v. 9). But like the father went to meet his son (Luke 15: 20), Jesus initiated a conversation with the woman (John 4: 7) and gave her the gift of grace (v. 10). The exchange between the woman and Jesus showed that she was not only surprised that he spoke to her, but also grateful that he genuinely cared about her as an individual (vv. 9, 14, 15). Despite her past, and how she was currently living (vv. 17-18), instead of condemnation, judgment, and rejection, the woman received acceptance. Having felt valued by Jesus, the woman was so excited that she told everyone about the amazing man who accepted her despite knowing everything about her (vv. 28, 29, 39).

Today, who are the Samaritans among us? Regardless of what religious, cultural, and societal traditions have said about ignoring certain people or treating them unjustly, whom can we intentionally and unconditionally accept?

COMPASSIONATE

As a child, I was baffled when people repeatedly said, "I'm grateful that he's the God of a second chance!" How could one person say this over and over again? Couldn't we receive a second chance only once? Why weren't they grateful for another chance?

As an adult, two scriptures helped me to understand that a second chance, not another chance, was in fact accurate. Micah 7: 19 and Psalm 103:8-12:

> *Once again you will have compassion on us. You will trample our sins under your feet and throw them into the depths of the ocean.*

> *The Lord is compassionate and merciful, slow to get angry and filled with unfailing love. He will not constantly accuse us, nor remain angry forever. He does not punish us for all our sins; he does not deal harshly with us, as we deserve. For his unfailing love toward those who fear him is as great as the height of the heavens above the earth. He has removed our sins as far from us as the east is from the west.*

These scriptures show that when we sin and ask for forgiveness, that's exactly what God does (I John 1: 9). Further, he does not keep a record of our mistakes. In other words, when God forgives, he forgets. Whereas another chance highlights that we have once again missed the mark, a second chance conveys that we have fallen, asked for forgiveness, and are starting anew. Friends, because of grace, we are always on our second chance.

Today, do you know someone who deserves a second chance? Perhaps we owe ourselves a second chance. If you don't know, ask the Lord to show you. And when he does, ask him for grace that forgives and forgets.

EVERLASTING

Of all its qualities, I am most grateful that grace is everlasting. It's eternal. It never runs out. Not only does grace exist because God loves us, it's also as infinite as his love for us. As nothing can separate us from the love of God (Romans 8: 38-39), nothing can take us beyond the grace of God.

Whenever we feel that we don't have anything to be thankful for, we can always be grateful for grace that endures and is everlasting. Despite not always having enough to provide for our families, grace still gives. For those who are estranged from loved ones, be encouraged because grace still restores. Though subjected to racism, classism, sexism, xenophobia, homophobia, and numerous systemic injustices, grace still accepts. And despite what we've done, grace remains compassionate and always gives us a second chance.

Happy Thanksgiving.

PERSONAL REFLECTION AND MEDITATION

1. What can you do to be an instrument of grace that gives to those who have been marginalized by systemic oppression?

2. What can you do to be an instrument of grace that restores broken relationships?

3. What can you do to be an instrument of grace that accepts those who do not look like you or believe what you believe?

4. What can you do to be an instrument of grace that is compassionate when others have hurt you?

5. What can you do to be an instrument of grace that is everlasting, especially when it is uncomfortable and inconvenient?

Thank you for grace. Help me to extend the same grace to others that has been freely, generously, and voluntarily given to me. Amen.

END OF
THE YEAR

HE IS OUR PEACE

*"Look! The virgin will conceive a child! She will give birth to a son,
and they will call him Immanuel, which means 'God is with us.'"*

Matthew 1: 23

In 1963, Andy Williams released Eddie Pola's and George Wyle's "It's The Most
Wonderful Time of The Year."[27] Today, it continues to be a Christmas anthem
of sorts—a popular song that is played while shoppers crowd malls, fill their
carts, and empty their coffers of treasure. But what makes the days anchored
between Thanksgiving and January 1st the most wonderful time of the year? Is
it the excitement of presents awaiting us under the tree? Is it the anticipation of
the close of a year that was fraught with circumstances that seemed to frustrate
us more than develop our faith in and dependence on God? Is it the dawning
of a new year that is filled with possibility and promise?

Lest we forget the Christ of Christmas, consider Isaiah's prophetic declara-
tion: *For a child is born to us, a son is given to us. The government will rest on his
shoulders. And he will be called: Wonderful Counselor, Mighty God, Everlasting
Father, Prince of Peace.* (Isaiah 9: 6). Further still, Matthew writes this comforting truth: *"The virgin will conceive and give birth to a son, and they will call him
Immanuel" (which means "God with us")* (Matthew 1: 23; New International
Version). From these passages it is clear that even before his birth, the Christ of
Christmas had purpose. And having been predestined with purpose, even his
name was purposeful. Now that we find ourselves in this season of perpetual
hope, love, and joy, let's also be mindful of another central theme that undeniably makes this the most wonderful time of the year: the peace of God.

Perhaps this year has been anything but peaceful. For those who are concerned about issues of equity and justice, the reality of systemic racism and
structural oppression against the poor, disenfranchised, and other marginalized
groups at times cause us to wonder, where is the peace? But although we don't

always feel his presence, we remember his name: God with Us.

Of all of the wonderful elements of the Christmas story, there is none more comforting than the Christ-child's humble entrance into the world. Amidst the controversial circumstances of being born to a young mother and unmarried parents (Matthew 1: 18-24), his arrival continues to speak peace to our lives and situations. Jesus was born outdoors amongst animals in a Bethlehem manger. But despite these things, we have peace because the most significant person in history, who was literally born into a situation that was far less than ideal, remains with us today.

As a child, I vividly remember that my pastor's favorite passage of scripture was Psalm 46. In only 11 verses, the psalmist confidently declares that regardless of his present circumstance, he is not alone because God is with him. Despite the impending attacks against his city (e.g., wars and rumors of war), there is no need to fear because God is with him. Hastening to the end, the psalmic division comes to a climatic close with this most-powerful and concluding verse: *The Lord* of Hosts is *with us; the God of Jacob is our refuge.* As it was then, so it is today: the ever-present help in times of trouble is Jesus: God with Us.

May you and your loved ones be overwhelmed with the peace of the Christ of Christmas, today and forevermore.

PERSONAL REFLECTION AND MEDITATION

1. Use this space to write your thoughts and reflections on this essay.

2. What was especially meaningful to you?

3. How can you ensure that you are continually experiencing the peace of the Christ all year long?

Thank you for always being my peace. Amen.

THE YEAR IN REVIEW: GO BACK ANOTHER WAY

Although going back another way will likely be inconvenient and filled with uncertainty, let's embrace all that God will show us as we do things differently.

For me, Christmas is the most wonderful time of the year. Amongst the reasons that are too numerous to name, I particularly enjoy the sounds of the season. Released in 1971 by John Lennon and Yoko Ono, "Happy Christmas," which is also known as "War is Over," includes the following lyrics: *So this is Christmas and what have you done? Another year over and a new one just begun.*[28] Coupled with enjoying quality time with family and friends, Christmas is an opportunity to reflect on all that we've experienced over the past 12 months. So friends, what have we done this year?

In the opening pages of the New Testament, Matthew chronicles the genealogy and birth of Christ (chapter 1). Chapter 2 (vv. 1-12) presents the account of wise men who travelled from the east to worship the newborn king. After following the star for several years that led them to the house in which Jesus was with his mother, the wise men worshipped and gave him gifts. Although worship and giving are certainly important, let's focus on the significance of verse 12 (English Standard Version): *And being warned in a dream not to return to Herod, they departed to their own country by another way.*

ADJUST THE PLAN, BUT DON'T ABANDON THE GOAL

What happens when we find ourselves in the last 30 days of the year having not done as much as we had hoped?

We likely feel discouraged. But instead of abandoning our goals, we should adjust our plans. Especially when we are confident that the Lord spoke to us about what we should do, unexpected setbacks are not indications to stop pursuing our goals. In fact, these delays are better understood as opportunities to refine and revise our strategy rather than giving up on what God has charged us to do. And because life, especially the Christian life, is always about growth, the frustration of deferred dreams could be God's way of developing our Christian character (Galatians 5:22-23).

When the wise men were told to go back another way, very importantly, they were returning home. In other words, their destination hadn't changed but the method by which they would get there was different. Because of this, going back another way was also a test of their faith. Instead of simply retracing their steps via the familiar route, the instruction to take a different path was to ensure that they were depending on God rather than their own abilities or astrological acumen (2 Corinthians 5:7). Although the star led them to Jesus, God would direct their path home.

So friends, be encouraged. Yes, we might not have accomplished everything that we intended this year. But instead of throwing in the towel, let's change our current practices so that next year is not another year of business as usual. Although going back another way will likely be inconvenient and filled with uncertainty, let's embrace all that God will show us as we do things differently. In fact, in order to have what we've never possessed, we must do what we've never done.

LIFE AFTER WORSHIP

As church attendance, membership, and participation in religious activities become increasingly common indicators of professing our faith, many Christians are complacent with such superficial engagement. But there is much more to Christianity—not as a way of doing, but as a way of living. Like the wise men, worship has, and will always be, central to our relationship with Christ. But worship is more than bowing and bringing gifts. Worship is our life and service.

Could it be that the directive to return by another route was to show the wise men that there is more that needs to be done after seeing Jesus? In other words, they came to the house, worshipped, and gave gifts to Jesus. Some would say that this was enough because they were in the presence of the king. But experiencing the presence of God is only the beginning. What happens afterwards?

Have we been changed and challenged to live differently amongst our sisters and brothers? Do we pursue peace according to Matthew 5:9 and Hebrews 12:14? Are we committed to living the Gospel, which is plainly articulated in Luke 4:18?

Going back another way is important because there will always be more that God wants to show us and accomplish through us. Without a doubt, there are people along this different path that need our encouragement. Through our actions, others need to know and experience that we have indeed been in the presence of the king.

As we embark upon a new year, I pray that we would not be limited by what has worked in the past, but obedient to the ever-speaking voice of God that perpetually provides all that we need.

PERSONAL REFLECTION AND MEDITATION

1. Use this space to write your thoughts and reflections on this essay.

2. What was especially meaningful to you?

Thank you for always having more to show me. Help me to embrace change, new experiences, and new ways of doing things. As I learn to trust you more each day, continue to increase my faith. Amen.

NEVERTHELESS

Simply defined as in spite of, nevertheless is a transitional term that announces what is going to happen regardless of what has already happened.

Recorded in Matthew (4: 18-22), Mark (1: 16-20), and Luke (5: 1-11), Jesus calls a few fishermen to be his first followers. Notably, Luke's perspective includes details not captured in the other accounts, especially the following: *we worked hard all last night and didn't catch a thing* (v. 5). Moreover, the subsequent clause contains one of the most pivotal words in the King James Version of the Bible: nevertheless. Especially at the end of the year, what is the significance of nevertheless?

THEIR FRUSTRATION

When Simon Peter said that he and his fellow fishermen *worked hard all last night* (v. 5), this could have been a literal retelling of their efforts. But more importantly, the statement conveys that they had toiled tirelessly without success. It is synonymous with consistently and diligently pursuing our goals since January, yet having less than what we had hoped for in December.

Perhaps most frustrating to the fishermen was the fact that they were professionals. They knew how to fish. But despite their expertise, on this particular day, they were unsuccessful. Further, they were likely discouraged because what felt like failure happened in an area of competence. How could I not be successful when I have earned degrees in this field? How could I not be successful when I've been doing this for so many years? Although these emotions and questions are reasonable, be encouraged. When we find ourselves in these situations, remember that God's timing is not our timing (2 Peter 3: 8) and his ways are not our ways (Isaiah 55: 8). In fact, the fishermen's seemingly futile night was less about catching fish than developing their patience and Christian character (Galatians 5: 22-23).

As we approach the close of another year, let's not allow what feels like failure to frustrate and discourage us. Although uncomfortable, these experiences are necessary to propel us toward what God has for us. Like Simon Peter, Andrew, James, and John, we are competent in what we have been trying to accomplish. However, something is missing and preventing us from experiencing the success that we desire.

THEIR FAITH

"Now go out where it is deeper, and let down your nets to catch some fish" (v. 4). Not only are yesterday's blueprints and past successes insufficient for tomorrow's opportunities, they can also be crippling if we become complacent and stagnant. Because these men's lives were on the brink of change, how they did things, including fishing, also had to be different.

Importantly, although Jesus directed the men to fish in deeper water, what they were doing did not change. In other words, where they were working was different. Reflecting on the areas in which we were less successful than we had hoped to be, like the fishermen, perhaps we were looking for success in a place that was no longer fruitful for us. No doubt, they had previously caught fish in shallow water; but it was time for them to use their abilities in deeper water.

Simon Peter's confidence in Christ led him to follow his instructions despite being a less experienced fisherman. And this, friends, is the embodiment of faith: trusting [someone] enough to do what may challenge our intellectual understanding (2 Corinthians 5: 7). For the fishermen, faith was the missing element to their success. When Simon Peter trusted Jesus by doing what he had likely never done before, he also experienced something for the first time: ... *the nets were so full of fish they began to tear* (v. 6)!

Is the Lord leading you to use your gifts in different places? Is he showing you other ways to accomplish your goals? As we embark upon a new year, let's not only develop our ability to discern what The Lord is saying to us, but also the courage to be obedient to his instructions.

THEIR FRIENDS

Simon Peter's affirmative and faith-filled response was not only life changing for him personally, but also his friends. Verses 7 and 10: *A shout for help brought their partners in the other boat, and soon both boats were filled with fish and on the verge of sinking… His partners, James and John, the sons of Zebedee, were also amazed.* Nevertheless led these men to a place in which they could not contain the overwhelming abundance that was awaiting them. Like Simon Peter, obedience will not only positively affect our own lives, but those close to us as well.

THEIR FUTURE

The Lord interrupts our lives to ultimately change the world. Because of nevertheless, an ordinary day, which followed a difficult and disappointing night, four men were intimately involved in altering the course of history (vv. 10-11).

Simply defined as in spite of, nevertheless is a transitional term that announces what is going to happen regardless of what has already happened. As we stand on the precipice of a year that is filled with new opportunities and possibilities, I pray that we would grow to nevertheless: a place of total surrender to the will and plan of God for our lives. Despite our fears and frustrations, let nevertheless, an unwavering trust in Christ, be our only resolution.

PERSONAL REFLECTION AND MEDITATION

1. In light of *New Year, New Season: Begin with the End in Mind* (p. 7), how are you doing with accomplishing your goals?

2. Regardless of what you have accomplished to date, what do you do well, but need to approach differently?

3. Because deeper water could also represent something that was more challenging and a place in which the fishermen would need to depend more on Christ, in what areas of your life are you too comfortable?

4. Why might the Lord be telling you to try something that is somewhat intimidating for you?

---•●•---

Thank you for choosing me to change the world. Thank you for using my gifts in ways that I cannot imagine. Increase my faith so that I will always follow your direction. Help me to grow to the place in which I am totally surrendered to your plan for my life. Amen.

---•●•---

ENDNOTES

1. Covey, Stephen R. *The 7 Habits of Highly Effective People: Powerful Lessons in Personal Change.* Simon & Schuster, 2013.

2. Covey, Stephen R. *The 7 Habits of Highly Effective People: Powerful Lessons in Personal Change.* Simon & Schuster, 2013, p. 98.

3. Kwapis, Ken, director. *He's Just Not That into You.* Flower Films, 2009.

4. Behrendt, Greg and Tuccillo, Liz. *He's Just Not Into You: The No Excuses Truth To Understanding Guys.* Simon Spotlight Entertainment, 2004.

5. Seuss, Theodor. *Horton Hears a Who!* Random House, 1954.

6. Seuss, Theodor. *Horton Hears a Who!* Random House, 1954, p. 1.

7. Hayward, Jimmy and Martino, Steve, directors. *Horton Hears a Who/Everyone's Hero.* 20th Century Fox, 2008.

8. Dickens, Charles. *A Tale of Two Cities.* Vintage Books, 1990, p. 1.

9. The Byrds. "Turn! Turn! Turn! (To Everything There Is A Season)." *The Bitter and the Sweet,* Columbia Records, 1962.

10. Franklin, Kirk. "Love." God's Property from Kirk Franklin's Nu Nation, Dallas, TX, 1997.

11. Warner, Anna Bartlett. *Say and Seal.* J.B. Lippincott, 1860.

12. Sorge, Bob. *Exploring Worship: A Practical Guide to Praise & Worship.* Oasis House, 2001.

13. Jones J, Mosher WD. Fathers' involvement with their children: United States, 2006-2010. National health statistics reports; no 71. Hyattsville, MD: National Center for Health Statistics. 2013.

14. Barrett, Pat et al. "Good Good Father." Never Lose Sight, Atlanta, GA, 2014.

15. Chapman, Gary. *The 5 Love Languages: The Secret to Love That Lasts.* Northfield Publishing, 2015.

16. "Founders Online: John Adams to Abigail Adams, 3 July 1776." National Archives and Records Administration, founders.archives.gov/documents/Adams/04-02-02-0016.

17. Sorge, Bob. *Exploring Worship: A Practical Guide to Praise and Worship.* Oasis House, 2001.

18. Niemöller, M. "First They Came for the Socialists..." United States Holocaust Memorial Museum, www.ushmm.org/wlc/en/article.php?ModuleId=10007392.

19. Hord, Shirley M. and Sommers, William A. "Leading Professional Learning Communities: Voices from Research and Practice." Corwin Press, 2007, p. 42.

20. King, Martin Luther. *A Letter from Birmingham Jail.* 1968.

21. Lartey, Jamiles. "Police Officer Responds to Alton Sterling Shooting: 'I See What You All See'." The Guardian, Guardian News and Media, 7 July 2016, www.theguardian.com/us-news/2016/jul/07/police-officer-responds-alton-sterling-nakia-jones.

22. Cropanzano, Russell and Ambrose, Maureen L. "The Oxford Handbook of Justice in the Workplace." *The Oxford Handbook of Justice in the Workplace,* Oxford University Press, 2015, p. 235.

23. King, Martin Luther. *A Letter from Birmingham Jail.* 1968.

24. Staples, Brent. "Just Walk on by: A Black Man Ponders His Power to Alter Public Space." *Ms. Magazine*, July 1986, pp. 50–52.

25. Mrs. Ackley. "When God Is in The Classroom." *Mrsackley.wordpress.com*, Wordpress, 8 Feb. 2017, mrsackley.wordpress.com/2017/02/08/classroom-god-teacher.

26. Seuss, Theodor. *Horton Hears a Who!* Random House, 1954.

27. Andy Williams. "It's the Most Wonderful Time of the Year." *The Andy Williams Christmas Album*, Columbia Records, 1963.

28. Lennon, John and Ono, Yoko. "Happy Christmas." *This is Christmas*, Apple Records, 1971.

www.ingramcontent.com/pod-product-compliance
Lightning Source LLC
Chambersburg PA
CBHW062048080426
42734CB00012B/2593